CONTENTS

INTRODUCTION

Greetings. My name is Beatrice and I've worked as a Script Supervisor around the country for 17 years. My background is artistic and academic - I have made experimental short films and taught film history. For a lark I ended up on a commercial film set, and after 12 grueling unpaid hours, that night, in bed, I wept. With joy. "My people!"

As far as film production and crew goes, Script Supervising (to me) is one of the best seats in the house. After working in several different departments, and learning a bunch, an opportunity to sit next to the Director presented and presto! Though sometimes the chair is actually an apple box, or crammed in a backseat, or on the process trailer going backwards, or standing, perhaps tiptoeing, to see the monitor at the edge of the set. This crew position is often challenging, demanding, satisfying, and at times exhilarating. And occasionally, even a way of being, a form of service, transcendent.

So many hands and hearts coming together from different trajectories to cohesively create something new is a beautiful process, miraculous at times, and never the same thing twice. More often than not the intensity of film making, with long hours, sometimes close quarters, the time and budget restraints each department holds, can bring out the best and/or the worst in people. There can be a lot of pressure.

These pages are a quickish guide to film and video production, from the Script Supervisor's point of view – the nuts and bolts, and the brain part, with some pointers for being on set. There are Script Sup specifics but much of the information can fill in gaps for any one interested in learning about on set film production.

As far as Script Supervising goes, this book describes the American based system. It is important to know the protocol and basic procedures, so that software can be a tool and not the whole game plan. Weather, tricky locations, dead batteries and equipment failure are very real things that can call for pulling out that paper, pencil and ruler to save the day.

And I will be honest here on the first page. As solid, true and helpful this information can be, you are not going to learn how to be a Script Supervisor from a book or computer program. A lot can be learned, but you have to do it, whether working for free on a student film or even practicing at home.

If this is not what you wanted to hear please go to the back of the book for information about the refund policy.

OH, and you can keep up with the blog or contact me at scriptsoupcentral.com.

SO YOU WANT TO BE A SCRIPT SUPERVISOR?

Good choice! But perhaps I am biased. For me it feels like being at the center of the action, working with so many interesting people in so many ways. It's impressive when the Actors bring words on paper to life, seeing the details in the set design, or the care in the costumes selected, following amazing camera work, moody lighting (did you know you could light with SMOKE?), wild cranes, car rigs for driving shots, as well as fantastic stunts and special effects - I've seen buildings burn and cars flip and ancient ships pull up to the New World, high jumps, long falls and explosions and wow!

Oh wait, what does the Script Supervisor do in all this?

There are four major parts to Script Supervising that go hand in hand. In hand in hand. These are Set Presence, Prep and Breakdowns, Shots and Forms, and Continuity.

Set Presence

There is a set etiquette and production protocol standard, and the Script Supervisor plays a role in getting information to fellow crew members, as well as supporting the director and actors.

The Prep and Script Breakdown

Films are often shot out of story or scripted chronology, and the breakdown serves as a quick reference for continuity, location, time, characters and action. It also breaks the script down mathematically, scene by scene.

Describing the Shot and Organizing Forms

The script acts as Bible...or Torah or Koran or Gita or Tipit-aka or fill in with your tome of choice. Actual notes are taken each time a camera rolls, with shorthand information about each take, preferences of the Director, any boo boos or variations.

Continuity

Help to hide the edits by keeping track of actions, ward-robe, props, hairstyles, emotions, look lines and, because we film in out-of-order pieces, making sure that shtuff (and I mean shtuff) matches!

We utilize these facets simultaneously. Round that off with tips for negotiating and reminders for self care, and away we go!

If things sound a little foreign, fear not. By the end it should all tie together. Let's dig in.

ON SET PRESENCE

*THESE ARE THE PEOPLE IN
YOUR NEIGHBORHOOD*

Before filling in the details, it's important to understand what working on a film production means – with departments and roles, what a filming day entails, and how the Script Sup fits into it all.

We are a department of one. We don't have a work truck to hang out on, nor inside on set jokes with our (non-existent) Super Script Supervisor team, nor a co-Script Supervisor to call for back up, for a battery, for raingear or a potty break. We are self-contained, and yet no one is an island.

As part of our on set duties, we interact with almost every department. This is an opportunity for friendship, for service to others, and for help if needed!

Everybody and every project is different, and I present a general overview of who's who from the inside spiraling out on a Union show, based on Script Sup's interaction NOT on any person being more important than another. These are the people in the film neighborhood!

Script Sup often watches with Director and DP at video monitors. This can be at "video village" or by the DIT. At times a separate bank of monitors are dedicated to the Script Sup, but my preference is to be where I can hear the comments and Director's notes as we film.

DIRECTOR – She is the Captain of a ship navigating by map (script) and by stars (Actors), working to bring a diverse crew (with maybe a pirate or 2) across the production seas, perhaps battling to get enough of the pieces to work together in a way that tells her version of the story that's been charted out and aimed for. Land HO!

There is pressure of time, Writers, Producers, constant choices, unexpected weather, snafus of all shapes and sizes. There may or may not be any rehearsal time before filming. Oh Arr, thar be dragons! (I don't know where this sailing talk is coming from!) Point being, there's a lot on their plate, and we want to help make sure they don't choke or spill.

Support them with appropriate communication. Some Directors do not want to be your friend, do not want to talk about the weekend plans, or their kids. Some do, but let them set the tone of how personal, how fast. Balance – be pleasant, be yourself but remember this is work not social hour. Pay attention during rehearsal, keep track of how the Director describes the intended shooting plan, later remind them of shots that will cover the edit, help them in the way they need to bring their story to life. If they want to talk, listen. If they want you to sit somewhere else, sit somewhere else - if you catch boo boos and make **relevant** suggestions, most likely they will begin to warm up to you.

On a television show there can be a rotation of different Directors. I think of them as guests being dropped into the machine that already has its own style and flow. Be kind. Even if a Director behaves like a jerk. On top of filming pressures we never know what someone else is going through in real life. Despite privilege or posturing, someone may be going through hell. If a Director treats people like poop he must feel like poop and that's what he has to give. Sad! DON'T TAKE IT PERSONALLY, despite how it might feel in the moment. It's their poop, don't let it get you dirty, be kind, it will help everyone, especially yourself.

DP – DIRECTOR OF PHOTOGRAPHY– He sets much of the visual tone of the project with camera and lighting. The DP guides the shots toward the Director's vision, and comes up with a plan for Camera Operators, the Gaffer and Key Grip to accomplish that.

Watch for unintended shadows, light reflections, matte boxes, focus issues, bumps or wobbles, and gently mention them if the DP doesn't mention such boo boos first. If you can be cool with the DP, a DP can be cool with you, and give you a heads up on what and where the cameras are headed. If the show is moving fast you can miss what's coming up next while you are addressing another issue in the moment, so having a buddy that can fill you in helps!

And keep those eyes peeled. Some DPs won't be shy about messing up continuity for the sake of their lighting. Good grief, who put that lamp on the desk in the middle of filming scene?

DIT –DIGITAL IMAGING TECHNICIAN – As part of the camera department, the DIT downloads the data from camera to send to editorial, adjusts visual settings per the DP, and maintains a data workflow. These days DIT and Assistant will sometimes be in charge of setting up secondary monitors (in lieu of a Video Assist person). They also may send out a wireless feed that crew can watch what we're filming on their personal devices. DP sometimes likes to stay by the DIT monitors, so the Director will often want to stay there too, which means Script Supervisor more than likely will follow in tow. So a crowd hovers over the DIT person, computers and monitors while she's trying to work! Be considerate, give DIT room to do their job too, be appreciative. A Script

Sup might need help with playback, setting up some mini monitors closer to set, or even for spare batteries, who knows, be nice!

And don't touch the monitors. Point, look, no touch!

1st AD - ASSISTANT DIRECTOR – THE AD breaks down the script to create a shooting schedule of days, scenes, locations and actor availability. The AD preps with the Director to work out as many of the schematics as possible beforehand. During filming the AD keeps the ship afloat, works to keep filming segments within an allotted timeframe, announces what's going on, and acts as an extension of the Director getting who and what is needed in line, troubleshoots. The AD should be able to say what the shooting order is, what cameras are doing, and what part of the scene we are jumping to. And if there's time to run to the bathroom!

Often a **2nd AD** stays by the monitors to keep an eye on background action, as well as assist the Director, DP or Script Sup in relaying messages to correct or improve the shot. Another 2nd AD also holds down the fort (base camp) dealing with logistics off set, like call sheets and cast needs.

PAs – PRODUCTION ASSISTANTS are ADs of the future. They are true helpers, "locking up" a set when rolling, acting as go-fers, following orders. PAs hand out sides (script pages) in the morning, and call sheets at wrap. Sometimes they are on top of everything, sometimes they are still learning, but in a good position to see all the departments get 'er done. In some ways, Production leans most heavily on them. They have walkies and can radio for help if they don't know how to meet your needs. Assess who can help and who is still trying to figure out being on set! But always be kind, they are generally overworked and underpaid. Today's PA might be tomorrow's Producer!

CAMERA OP - Depending on the show and the crew, the DP may take the Camera Operator's suggestions as to placement or may tell each camera where to set up, what lens/setting to use, what camera control equipment to use for the shot. Each camera has its own unit of people dedicated to getting the assigned shot. The Operator makes the move - panning, tilting, zooming, tilting or keeping still, whether camera is handheld, on a tripod or on a rig.

1st AC – FIRST ASSISTANT CAMERA - actually pulls the focus on the camera or remotely at a monitor. ACs also handle lens changes and adjustments to camera bodies and mounting the camera on the stand.

2nd AC supports the team by reloading the camera, slating the shot, keeping on top of batteries, camera adjustments and some heavy lifting too. They drop marks on to the floor during rehearsals so the actors remember where to stand or stop on a move (for focus).

If there's no monitor the Script Sup should take a peek through the lens once the camera's set up to see the composition and what characters will be in the shot. Just ask nicely. If there are no monitors except the one the 1st AC is pulling focus from, if you are cool with them they might just share the view with you.

It's best to have very clear communication with the 2nd ACs. We tell them or confirm as to what to put on the slate, and watch those slates for errors. The slates are the markers that tell the editor what camera, what scene, what take and what set up the footage is for.

More on slating in a bit.

Each camera has an Operator, 1st AC and 2nd AC. On low/no budget one person might be doing it all.

VFX – VISUAL EFFECTS – These folks deal with the image in post-production. A big clue, if there's a literal green screen (though sometimes its blue) in the shot, they will be adding or changing something in the picture with computer magic. It's handy to add a "V" on the front of the slate number as an indicator, and often times there will be particular information to get from the 2nd AC concerning measurements and settings.

SOUND MIXER – The leader of the Sound Department is the Sound Mixer, who also slates for each sound take, records the action or dialogue and makes sure it sounds right. A **BOOM OPER-ATOR** or two follow dialogue over the Actors' heads with microphones mounted on poles. Good golly, can you imagine making a living by holding your arms up over your head all day long? Before rolling they usually place battery powered personal mics, lavalieres (lavs), on each Actor. Thus several streams of sound are recorded, mixed and captured.

Script Sup makes sure Sound has the correct slate as well, and watches for boom shadows and boom dipping in to frame. An Actor's lav, mic pack or wire might shift and show after few takes. Also an astute Mixer will often follow along with the script and might act as a second set of ears if there's a flub. They listen hard for planes, trains, horns, interruptions. Sound provides us with headphones. Be nice and you will get a good pair, maybe even with your name on it! Be kind to them and respectful of their equipment, and they will be kind and respectful in return. Sometimes we need to go back and listen to some dialogue, an adlib or how a line was delivered during a particular take, and if we are nice the Mixer will be more willing to help.

VIDEO ASSIST – These folks set up monitors for the village, and mini monitors for those that need to be closer to set. Full fledged Video Assist doesn't seem to automatically be on film sets as much and it breaks my heart. They record every take for instant playback. It is a blessing to easily see footage from moments ago or days ago, for matching or to grab a screenshot. It seems like this job has gotten mushed into filming digital notes for Script Sup, or imposed on the DIT department, who only gets the footage once the memory cards are out of the camera, so no instant replays unless through a camera, which is not an option.

ACTORS – Support support support, and sometimes that means leaving them alone! No harm in asking how to assist them. Check to see if the Director wants to be the one to deliver corrections when needed. In the wait time before rolling it might be good to ask Actors if they want to run lines. While rolling, gently correct them when they call for help, between takes remind them of important continuity moves if they seem to be missing their cues.

While rolling, Actors will ask for forgotten dialogue by saying "line," or the Director might have you call it out. Some shows want every word as written, some shows are open to interpretation.

Don't pick too much. Do it all with the intention of helping the Actors look good, meaning perfect for what the scene requires. They've got the whole world looking up their noses and in their teeth, as well as dozens of crewmembers and equipment and lights sometimes inches from their faces. Pressure! Be kind.

HAIR and **MAKE UP** - Sometimes called the Vanities, these two departments work closely together. It's not always about Actors looking beautiful, it takes work to make someone appear ill, dirty, injured, aged. There can be bruises or intentional messiness to keep track of as such affectations progress throughout the story (cuts to scars, levels of sweat). It helps to have extra eyes to confirm where these touches are in the timeline as we often film out of chronological story order.

Basic things that pop up are stray hairs or shiny spots on the face. It's helpful to know which Hair and which Make Up folks are working on a particular Actor if there's something to correct for the next take - instead of going through the ADs it might be quieter and quicker to go directly. And as friendships develop it's more about trust and help than corrections, isn't that better? To notice and care about Hair/Make Up's good work can encourage them to monitor the results take by take if for some reason they aren't already. In a big or busy scene, extra eyes watching hair continuity (left shoulder, right shoulder, back, front) is a big help!

WARDOBE – A COSTUME DESIGNER selects or creates the clothing to add to the character's portrayal and the story, so subtle and so powerful at the same time! A whole team buys, tailors, cleans, preps and checks wardrobe for the leads and the background actors too. Again, filming out of order there may be sweat, rips, dirt, as well as wardrobe changes to keep track of. The Set Costumers give the actors the appropriate outfits, make sure the correct number of buttons are open, sleeves rolled to the elbow, shirts tucked or untucked, etc... A Costumer may watch the set or be assigned to a specific Actor, so good to know who to tell directly about a fuzzy, weird wrinkle or anything distracting instead of making a big announcement through the ADs.

PROPERTY or Props – The PROP MASTER breaks down the script to find all the specific objects and object cues written into the story. Props handles just about any object the actors touch in a scene – cups, pens, clipboards, toothbrushes, knives, photo-graphs, bicycles, cell phones, food and wine for all those dinner scenes! Purses and sunglasses are a toss up with wardrobe. Props might build things that don't exist, or rig things to do what's written in the script, like light up, or break apart in a certain way (or this might be Special Effects too.)

Buying, making, and preparing occur with the hard work of the PROP ASSISTANTS, who are also the folks on set. Prop Assts have extra eyes to automatically watch for certain continuity (or be gently reminded) like reset cigarettes, refill water glasses, put the briefcase in the correct hand. If the show moves fast, it never hurts to check in with Props, and share any heads up of possible changes.

These kind souls also set up, over and over again, the director's chairs. Be appreciative, not expectant. If you are with Director and Actors on a different part of the set while the monitors, and thus the chairs, move, Props can toss your stuff on the ground, or kindly bring your script, your pad, your bag with them. Be nice.

ON SET DRESSER – These folks tweak the set that has been created and put in place by the Art Department. Set Dressers move furniture, hide cords, adjust pictures for the benefit of the camera, wipe stuff down or dust it up, basically make the set look real and appropriate in more ways than anyone would realize. Magicians, they can be. The On Set Dresser can tell you when the DP or a grown up has decided to fiddle with the already established set arrangement, and takes continuity pics to prove it!

CRAFT SERVICE – These Lifesavers provide beverages, snacks and, at times, actual come-and-get-it meals. Even though these people often bring tables, carts, coolers and trays of sustenance, they also have a trailer stocked with simple things you can make for yourself. Even so, sometimes Script Sup cannot break away to make that gluten free sandwich or tea with special sweetener. PAs can occasionally get a nibble for desperate you - appreciate every action and offer for help. Appreciate your Craft Service pals for being able to supply hot coffee and cool water in remote locations, and often they will help you with special dietary needs, or when you can't step off the set.

Craft Service is also called Crafty. They *do* need to be crafty in some locations and with smaller budgets! I mention it because Script Sup is often called Scripty. These are the only positions that get cutesy names. Directory? No. I try to roll with it when this old impersonal moniker is used, imagining it's said with endearment, but tis not my fave. Makes me feel like I'm wearing a diaper. Bah!

MEDIC - Speaking of Lifesavers, know who to call for immediately if there's an accident or illness involving someone else, or if you yourself feel like you are going down. Medics will have basic supplies, as band-aids and aspirin, but some will carry supplements and homeopathic products too. They are not to be used as the daily on set vitamin store, they are there to help crew with injury or illness. Some medics have also been EMTs and carry back boards and more hardcore emergency supplies and equipment. When all is running smoothly, they may seem to be sitting around, but know Medics are one of the first to arrive and one of the last to leave set as all the other crew loads in by morning then loads out at the end of the night.

TRANSPO – TRANSPORTATION Each department truck has a designated driver, but the people Script Sup sees most are the van drivers. It may seem easy to drive cast and crew from parking to base camp to set etc... but think of that responsibility when it's the end of a looong day, or bad weather, or over terrible terrain. Be nice, thank them for the ride, even though that's their job. Your life is in their hands! And who knows when your car battery might need a jump, or you need a quick run back to your car for dry socks!

ELECTRICS – The **GAFFER**, the Chief Electrician, follows the DP's lead to light the scene. A team of Electricians*, sometimes called Lighting Technicians, move and adjust the lights for brightness, size and even color (using gels – transparent colored sheets of heat resistant plastic). They also have hardy electrical cables, called stingers, and if in a pinch with nowhere to plug in a dying laptop, they may set you up with power or point you to a lunchbox (a power station cube of outlets). There can be a lot of Electricians working hard, but it costs nothing to say hello, and ask how their world is.

*In general these are not like the electricians that work for the electric company.

GRIPS – The **KEY GRIP** heads this department, and also follows the DP's instruction as to blocking the light, or controlling where light and shadow goes with silks, flags and reflective boards. They are the go-to guys for safety, in charge of securing stands, harnesses, and building rigs around cars for driving shots. This includes camera control, like setting up special mounts, or dolly track, and the dollies themselves. They are good with knots and seem the most like sailors with lines, fabric, wooden chocks. Grips often set up black courtesy flags at the monitors to block glare and make it easier to see. Thank you Grips a million times! And they are the keepers of the apple boxes, which have countless uses as seats, risers and stabilization. Here is where I go, to the Grips, asking to use an apple box to sit on when I must tuck in closer to the Actors. Never ask for a box to serve as an end table for drinks and snacks, this is a tool. Be thankful, be nice, what a gift when people help one another!

UNION STEWARD – A Union crewperson with steward training is selected to be eyes and ears while working their actual job on set on a show. They are supposed to keep production honest with times, turnarounds, penalties etc...and act as sort of mediators if an issue arises that would be under the Union's belt. I don't know about LA but in Texas if you call the Union office while filming at 4 in the morning, Bub, you are getting an answering machine. These folks will sometimes double-check their times with the Script Sup's.

ABOVE THE LINE – The Grown Ups. Back to Video Village for a moment. Sometimes **WRITERS** and **PRODUCERS**, who can be one and the same, will sit there as well. Above the line, meaning "above" the crew on the callsheet, same as with the Director. Be polite, let them set the tone of interaction, don't ask them to read your own screenplay right off the bat. But do approach them with a question or discrepancy regarding the script if the AD or Director can't answer. Know they have their own issues and pressures as well and that you are there to help, even by staying out of the way.

But not too out of the way, because the Script Supervisor has an important job to do as well.

There are more talented and amazing people doing what they do best, such as Stunts, Special Effects, Caterers, Accountants, Office Crew, and Post Production, but those highlighted above tend to be the folks we are in the on set frontlines with every day.

So many hands and hearts come together from different directions to cohesively create something new. This is a beautiful process, miraculous at times, and never the same thing twice. More often than not the intensity of film making, with long hours, close quarters, the time and budget restraints each department holds, can bring out the best and/or the worst in people. There can be a lot of pressure across the board.

We teach people how to treat us (mostly), by how we treat others and by what treatment we ourselves tolerate. What I expect of others is respect, because that is what I expect of myself to give.

Help people, be kind to mistakes and that kindness may be returned to you. Would you prefer to be called out and humiliated for a mistake, or politely corrected? Act accordingly. Do the best you can. That being said, I think crew would prefer to work with someone pleasant and supportive, good at their job but human, rather than someone standoffish, self-important, militant, correct and overcorrecting all the time.

This isn't about being nice to people so they will do us favors, but to be present, to exchange good spirited energy to create more, to expand our hearts and inspire a sense of service. Seemingly small acts or thoughts can lift someone up. Movie making, being a cashier or a CPA, whatever job you invest your time into, remember it's not just work, it's life in the moment.

And yet...be aware and beware of inappropriate behavior on set. Anyone can get cranky, exhausted, dehydrated and act grouchy. Misunderstandings happen. Some of us naturally use what we consider non-threatening touch when we speak or tell a story. OK, but if someone is downright inappropriate with touch or language you do not have to sit there and smile about. Tell them no. Sometimes a not so cool conversation happens beside you in earshot. Distance yourself from them. If it seems targeted at you and persists, tell the Union Steward, tell the studio, tell the biggest Producer you can find. If you need to leave the project for your safety leave the damn project, no job is worth as much as you and your safety.

So let's aim to play well together!

CRAM FOR THE COVID TEST

By the way...via the Union and Guilds, the film industry has developed a covid protocol to be able to proceed with productions. A new department has been formed for creating and implementing a covid plan for testing, monitoring, distribution of PPE and some extra clean up. Union shows, Indies and Commercials seem to apply levels of this protocol as appropriate to their project.

Basically there is an initial covid test 1-2 days before first arriving on set (Union shows compensate for folks taking this first test). This test can be the deep swab, the soft swab or, ladies and gentlemen, I have just recently seen the spittle test. After an initial negative result, a new routine begins each day of work.

A daily health survey is emailed out, and must be answered and returned before arriving on the job. Then once at base camp or the set location, if the questionnaire has been approved, there is a daily temperature check, and another covid test based on your assigned 'zone.'

Production began categorizing crew positions through a zoning system based on proximity to the shooting set, or Actors, so A zone crew undergoes more covid testing than B or C zone. Check-in lines, transportation, bathrooms and catering areas are also designated by these separate zone classifications.

Passenger vans are fairly empty for spacing riders out, and lunch, well, bring a megaphone. Or ping pong paddle.

Filming days are supposed to be shorter to accommodate

for the extra procedures, deeper clean up and to let crews get more rest.

Good luck everybody.

I have avoided adding this little chapter or enfolding this information into the film flow portion of this book for months in hoping this wouldn't have lasted so long in the world. And I still hope these are temporary measures, and that sooner than later film family can get back to more normal including smiles, hugs and sitting side by side.

But maybe we can keep up with the regular cleaning of those bathroom doorknobs! And now back to the book.

ON SET AND BEYOND

What's a typical day like? We'll flesh out the details throughout the book but here's a run-down. It starts the night before, when a **call sheet**, basically a schedule of the scenes to be shot, comes out for the next filming day. The front side lists the work – the scenes, the Actors involved, the locations, any special props, equipment or effects that are needed, and a general crew time to report on set. Often there is an advance little peek of what is scheduled for the next day as well. The back of the call sheet lists the departments with crew member names, and any different call times. Always double check!

The Script Supervisor prepares for the next shooting day by looking at the scheduled scenes - rereading them, perhaps the scenes leading up to them and the closest scenes before and after that the characters are in, noting any special props or continuity, pulling up pictures to match an established costume or look - doing whatever can be done ahead.

Here's how the wheel goes round and round. By the end of this book you will better understand this routine!

OK let's prepare for a 7am **call time** - ready on set - and an 8:00 am shooting call - begin filming by 8:00am.

Fix intentions – that everyone has a safe day on set, that the work goes smoothly, and that it's fun! Choose how you want your day to go.

Arrive early enough to **travel** to set from parking, sometimes a van ride. Factor in breakfast at catering before call as well.

Greet people as you go! Especially the grumps.

ON SET

Get to set before call, and grab a set of **sides** from a PA. Sides are a mini-version, half-page size, of the day's scenes only, not the whole script. Even for those working digitally, sides are a great light weight way to follow dialogue, track continuity per take, and show an Actor a line during a scene.

It's good to double check that the sides are correct, and include all the scenes from the day's work. I prefer the Texas sized, full-page sides for less eye-strain and more room to make notes.

At 7:00 am - we're in, we're in! Cell phones off please. Now (in theory) there is a **rehearsal** of the scene with Actors, which can be a walk through to get the basic action down, called **blocking**. Marks of Actor's movements may be placed on the floor as reference. Using a different color per Actor, the marks can be tape or little T-shaped sandbags. Actors are sent back to Make Up and **Stand-Ins** take their place at those marks, so the cameras and Electricians have a subject to work with.

OR there may not be a rehearsal but a **shooting plan** laid out. It never hurts to ask if there is a **shot list**, prepared ahead of time by the Director. Either way, **cameras and lights** are set up, as well as other departments tucking in their areas near set.

For Director, Producers, DP and Script Supervisor some sort of monitors and chairs are set up – the Video Village. These folks watch from other monitors at times.

When the technical part is ready the **Actors are invited** to set. They will be **wired** with personal lavaliere microphones (called lavs or mics) for sound if needed.

Script Supervisor makes sure Sound and 2nd ACs know the

scene number for their slates, and confirms the sound and camera "rolls" they are on. Check camera slate for correct date and other information. Make sure there's a Comtek (headphones or sound receiver) on the script chair, or ask for one when visiting Sound Department friends.

A final rehearsal or walk through may take place now. **Last looks** (hair, make up, wardrobe tweaks, props given) and we're set to roll. Well more than likely the equipment is digital, no longer using rollers to move strips of film or audio tape around, but this is the lingo.

Breathe!

AD – **"Lock it up!"** meaning PAs (Production Assistants) guard the perimeters of the set, and also for everyone to be quiet. **"Let's roll!"** The PAs will call out "rolling" for all to hear and make sure no one wanders in during filming.

First **Sound** calls out **"speed"** when they are rolling and the recording machine is up to speed (remember this used to be analog, mechanical rollers, and tape).

Then **Cameras** call out **"speed"** when they are rolling and ready. ACs can now **slate**, announcing what the scene and take number is, then shut the slate or clapper board in front of each camera rolling. In editorial, the start of this clap on the sound roll would be lined up to the film frame of the clapper arm just hitting the board, to synchronize sound and picture. Today this system is perhaps a back up, for the **timecode** (hour minute seconds frame) on the slate is used to **sync** up to the timecode on the sound file. SO the editor will only have to match up numbers.

During a sound take, if the camera slates but sound missed it, they call for "second sticks" and the Camera AC reslates. If the camera missed the slate or was unable to get one in before rolling, aim to get a **tail slate**, named so because it's placed at the end of the take, before the camera and sound cut. The clapper is placed upside down as an extra indicator marking the end of the take for the editors. Isn't that smart?

Director calls out "**action!**"

The AD may **repeat "action!"** to make sure the cue is heard.

Script Supervisor notates the clock time of the **first shot** of the day (remember production was aiming for an 8:00am shooting call) then starts **timing the shot.**

Actors **act.**

Script Supervisor **follows** lines, actions, any continuity. Watches for boo boos as camera shadows, boom dipping in, bumpy dolly move, flubbed lines.

Director calls out changes and keeps rolling, or calls out "**cut!**"

AD may call "**cut!**" as well. PAs follow suit and release the lock up.

Script Supervisor stops timing, **notates** slate, set up, time and specific take information, lines the script page, tells 2nd AD the clock time of the first shot (what time 'action' was first called for the day) and notes it on Lunch Report and Daily Progress Report.

Any notes from the Director? Corrections? Changes? Print (AKA Circle - literally draw a circle around the take number in the notes showing it's a keeper) this take?

Next take. When Director is satisfied, cameras change position or framing, becoming a **new camera set up,** on and on until there is enough coverage to edit this scene.

End scene.

Then on to the **next scene**, rehearsal, set up, roll, change the shot...

When a camera reloads the "film roll," more than likely a memory card, Script Sup eventually borrows the **camera report** from that camera's 2nd AC to check for slating boo boos, to circle takes the Director liked, and to glean info for the notes like lens settings. Return checked report to the 2nd AC or DIT. This is standard procedure.

AD calls "**lunch!**"

Script Supervisor **notes time** that lunch is called for the Lunch Report and Daily Report. Lunch is typically scheduled 6 hours after crew call, 1:00 pm in this example. If finishing up a shot that then runs over the 6 hour mark, Grace may be called, allowing for a few minutes past the 6 hour mark to complete the set up. If a camera changes position or a lens for a new take, essentially making a new shot, then this grace period has been broken. If broken, or grace is not called at all, the time delaying lunch becomes a meal penalty, a little bump in pay.

Script Supervisor prepares a **Lunch Report** for the ADs, listing what has been filmed so far – the scenes completed, the scenes partially filmed, page count, minutes and number of set ups. The clock time of the 1st shot, as well as the time lunch was called also goes on the Lunch Report.

If there is a **film break**, the morning's sound files and camera footage is sent to editorial, and Script Supervisor sends or emails a **copy of the Shot List**.

Preliminary call sheets (prelims) for the next day often come out at lunch. This can change, but serves as advance notice of what scenes the various departments should begin to prepare for, and is an opportunity for departments to clarify with Production if adjustments, special equipment or additional manpower is needed. As Script Supervisor I **check the page count** and Day/ Night listed for each scene with my own breakdown. If it differs I will politely share the discrepancy with the AD building the call sheet and they can choose to make corrections for the official call sheet.

"We're back in!"

Sometimes it's back to the same set. Sometimes there's a company move to another location, which allows time for crew to drive or shuttle elsewhere. All the equipment needs to be loaded, transported and unloaded again. Company moves can happen any time of the day.

After lunch we do it again for another 6 hours, hence ideally a 12-hour production day.

Script Sup notes the time of the **first shot after lunch** on the **Daily Report**, tells 2nd AD.

The AD calls **"wrap"** at the end of the day. The crew packs up the equipment. Very few people just leave, unless work begins in the same spot the next day, then the equipment can stay put. In that situation everything is made safe then it is considered a **walk away**.

Call sheets for the next day are handed and emailed out.

Script Sup **notes wrap time**, also called camera wrap. Script Sup's own wrap out involves condensing the day's work – scenes completed, partial scenes, number of set ups, page count and minutes – and folding those numbers into a running tally on the **Daily Progress Report**. Double check the numbers! ADs need a copy of the DPR before leaving work. Times for first shot, lunch, first shot after lunch and camera wrap are listed. So are scenes completed and page count completed. It's also important to list special remarks, as owed shots or wildlines.

Ideally before leaving for the night, copies of the full day's script notes with DPR and Daily Shot Lists are **sent to editorial**, and the Office. (Often, so long as ADs get the DPR it can be acceptable to finish organizing and send out the day's notes from home. Some shows want the notes ASAPPP, and some shows do not have editors working through the night, and can wait a few momentos.

Yes! **Go home!** Have a bite, have bath, have a glass of wine or cup of cocoa...

No wait, it's not over yet. The priority is to organize and send in the script notes from that day if this wasn't done at set. Then the Script Supervisor can have a relaxed rest of the **wrap out** at home, like printing or organizing the days continuity photos, making detailed notes for self in the breakdown, organizing script pages, and **prepping for the next day**, once again going over the scheduled scenes, pulling pictures and preparing forms. Typically an hour of pay is allocated for this wrap out/prep time.

If a **script revision** has been released, with changes that would affect the breakdown, then the breakdown should also be revised and sent out. If the show is a killer with a puny turnaround it may not be realistic to complete, but be aware of any big changes that cannot wait until completing the revision.

12-HOUR DAY???

The standard 12-hour day of production time does not include lunch. The half hour allotted on the books for lunch may actually take longer so that the last crew person, or "last man" in the lunch line can have a full half hour lunch. Calling a 12-hour day a 12-hour day does not include prep nor the time it actually takes to pack out the equipment nor typical travel. So a day with a 7:00am call would casebook aim to have a 7:30 pm wrap, but after wrap folks keep working on the clock to pack out.

A Union contract guarantees a minimum turnaround time (8 -10 hours) for crew after wrap to ensure we don't film til midnight, then begin at 7 am the next day. However in the big picture scrum and chase (to get out of a location, to shoot an Actor out, to keep from adding another day of filming) turnaround times can get crunchy, especially with departments that might have to come in early, like Hair / Make Up if an Actor has to be camera ready at call. There are penalties, bumps in pay, which are small bumps for crew, big bumps if an Actor's turnaround is forced. So even with a 12-hour shootinday, at wrap, the crew still works at wrangling cables, tearing down cameras, collecting props and loading up the trucks.

Again, Script Supervisor sends copies of the day's notes off, at least the DPR, but then can finish wrapping out, and prepare for the next day, from home. Factor in wrap out, lunch hour and travel time, and a standard 12-hour shooting day can, in reality, be closer to 14-15 hours devoted to film work.

Thus, it is in your best interest to **love what you are doing** and love some aspect of the project you are a part of. As much as possible. Some shows are a dream come true, some a nightmare. When it's tricky, focus on something special, as a kindness given or accepted, or the camaraderie in the whole crew muddling through. Save that favorite CD or podcast for the drive home! Seems counter intuitive but when I put myself more deeply into my duties, the insane Director or filthy location fades into the background. Perhaps this is a way to **be present** even in trying circumstances.

And remember, we are **choosing** to do whatever we are doing in the moment. Different choices may have different consequences but they're all choices despite what we consider our "shoulds" and "gottas."

So when choosing to be on a Production, time and energy are precious. To streamline wrapping out, getting ready for the next day's scenes, and having a checks and balance system of organization, before filming begins the Script Supervisor has a period of Preparation.

YE OLDE PREP

Breakdowns and Timing

Before filming begins there is a period of Pre-Production preparation, better known as Prep. At this time locations are scouted, a Production office opens, equipment is rented, sets built, and Actors are still being cast. There are camera tests, contracts, crew hires, costumes designed, hair and makeup decisions, stages prerigged for lighting, meetings meetings meetings...

Often the Script Supervisor is brought on for the weeks just before Production (actual filming) starts – a standard movie may offer 2 weeks of prep, Indies maybe a week, maybe they will push for less. The bigger the movie, the bigger the prep. Per episode, television may offer 2 days. If two Script Supervisors are not alternating episodes and it's just you, Jack, plan to work some weekends.

Occasionally the Script Sup will be invited to rehearsals and table readings. Clarify with Production if these are on the clock or voluntary, because this is the film and television *business*, and the Producer who hires you wants to spend as little money as he or she can get away with. More later on negotiating.

Script Sup's prep work breaks down the script into several specific streams of information that equal a whole, to be shared for Key meetings and Key crew. Although each department will benefit from referencing this fantastic breakdown, it serves as the Script Sup's very own guide in the inevitable darkness. See, movies almost always shoot out of story order due to locations, Actors' availability, time of year or even equipment. Night time scenes may be filmed by day, or the finale at the beginning of the shoot. So a good breakdown can be like a map that keeps everyone on course, maybe not lounging on the deck of the QE2, but at least aiming all collective department canoes toward the same general direction.

Several other departments make their own breakdown for their specific needs. Ours is the Master that must stay up to date as revisions (script changes) come out during production. The cleaner, clearer, and more orderly a breakdown, the better. For episodic TV the breakdown's condensed even further.

Hopefully the script is locked, meaning the scene and page numbers won't shift around with any revisions or changes made to the script pages. Sometimes the studio will release "drafts" and won't lock the script until the night before shooting begins.

That. Is. A. Drag. And extra work.

The breakdown relays broad strokes of information (as total number of scenes, total page count, total estimated running length) as well as specific info scene by scene. Throughout the production these numbers are used to keep tabs on what's been shot and what hasn't, what we have filmed and what we owe. Like ticking off debits and credits in a balanced checkbook against the bank statement.

Details are pulled from the scene headings and script pages – scene number, page count length of each scene, day or night, interior or exterior, location; and a description of the scene finishes it off. A breakdown acts as CliffsNotes, with quick references of information, as well as a reminder of the pieces of the puzzle to catch in all the hustle and all the bustle.

Generally Production requires the Script Sup to turn in 3 basic things during prep – the Day/Night Breakdown, the Script Breakdown, and the Timing. I enter data into my own simple documents created with office type software.

DAY/NIGHT BREAKDOWN

It helps to first create a basic Day/Night Breakdown by carefully reading the script for clues to track time. Other departments, like Wardrobe, appreciate getting this ASAP as they build (or compare ours with) their own breakdowns.

The D/N Breakdown lists how the scripted story falls in linear time, of what scenes go where in the story's timeline. This always follows numerical scene order and can be as simple as follows.

```
D=Day, N=Night, FB=Flashback

Sc.  1-5            D1

     6-7            D2

     8              N2

     9-14           D3

     15-16, 21      FBD1

     17-19          D4

     20             N5
```

Each scene heading in the script should say if a scene is day or night. Once in awhile a script will even state DAY 3 or NIGHT 5 in the scene heading. Even so by the time we get our little paws on the script, with revisions and rewrites, things can get mixed up. The heading may proclaim one thing but the story another. Read carefully, Script Sup Detectives catch inconsistencies. Also, scenes in the story can be out of linear order, so beware of Flash-backs.

DAY 1 and DAY 2 don't necessarily mean "Monday" then "Tuesday." The numbers serve as a reference to show that DAY 2 is literally a different story day, be it the "tomorrow" on the calendar, or weeks later. Each new DAY and NIGHT listed is a possible cue to establish new looks for hair, make up, wardrobe and props, which may be different from the previous DAY or NIGHT. Of course looks might change within a day, like in real life, but again the D/N Breakdown is a starting point.

Notice that although it is the first night scene shown in the D/N example, scene 8 takes place on NIGHT 2, meaning the action takes place the evening of the DAY 2 action. The numbers express the scene's place in chronology, not if it's the first, second or third night in the written script.

Flashback - We've all seen them in the movies, as a memory, revisiting an old family tale, or even a bit of world history. Generally a flashback represents a moment preceding the main story's bubble of time.

The film Citizen Kane operates with multiple flashbacks. Recluse elderly mogul Charles Foster Kane has died. A reporter assigned to write about him conducts interviews, which uncover details about Kane's childhood, schooling, business ventures, failed marriages and political endeavors. The viewer is shown his past in flashbacks rather than just told via the interviews. See it if you haven't yet!

SCRIPT BREAKDOWN

Here we chart Scenes, Page Count, Day/Night, Interior/Exterior, Location, Description, andTime. Now to really roll up our sleeves!

Look at a screenplay as an expressive outline, broken down into individual moments called scenes. Everything in the story must be on the script page, to be seen or heard, captured and expressed on the screen. There is no meandering in a characters mind or postulating over motivations as there might be in prose. Well, there shouldn't be. Perhaps a screenplay can be seen as a very well dressed skeleton.

The breakdown lists the scene heading information, story in time, and a brief description of each scene. In this the characters, special props or special actions should be noted.

One function of the breakdown concerns the numbers – how many scenes, the page count per scene and in total, keeping track of what's credited (completed) and what's owed.

Digital Script Supervising programs do much of the numbers part of the breakdown. For how *my* brain works, filling in by hand is part of the process of getting to know the script. Lay it out in any way that's clear, but perhaps across the board it's best to begin with the scene numbers.

SCENES

A scene indicates a complete section, of any length, in the stream of the story. Time and location can be indicators of a new scene, ideally motivated by moments. New location, new moment, new scene. Ah. A whole movie can be set in a banquet hall, one room, but actual scenes might take place at the wedding table, in front of the bar, by the kitchen doors. One scene might show throwing the bouquet on the dance floor, and with a time cut the next scene can be in the same spot after everyone's gone but the janitor, sweeping up confetti.

Scenes are numbered chronologically. Sequential order - 1,2,3,4. Simple! These number assignments do not change once the script is locked. But sometimes there are revisions, where scenes are edited, where scenes are added or deleted to the script, or the scene order is changed.

Added Scenes- If a scene is added to a locked script and inserted between scene 2 and scene 3 the numbers of all the other scenes don't shift up (because the script is locked, yo!), the new scene is called A3. If there are 2 new scenes between 2 and 3 they are called A3 and B3. Kinda sorta like the Dewey decimal system in that additions tuck in without having to renumber everything else already established. Added scene numbers **precede!**

Note proper form has the letter **BEFORE the scene number**, making for clearer slating when filming. That will make sense when we get to the Slate.

Omitted Scenes- Sometimes a scene is omitted, but it keeps its scene number. To show there's no clerical mistake, it's best to keep that scene number in the breakdown with "omitted" in the description area. Omitted scenes do not count toward the total number of scenes.

Shuffle - Sometimes a revision might move the scene order about and thus renumber. If the writer wants scene 4 to come in earlier, scenes 1,2,3,4 would become 1, 2, A3 (formerly scene 4), and 3, with 4 considered an omitted scene.

The breakdown lists all of the scene numbers, including the omitted scene numbers, but will reflect a tally only of the active scenes in the script. Again, omitted scenes are not included in this tally.

This record keeping is also a way to clarify when a scene is complete, and thus credited as complete, finito, or when a part of a scene is still owed and more must be shot later. I've worked with a notable director who gets hot A list Actors for his films, he just might not get them all at once, so we filmed one side of a conversation with Mr. X. The scene sat incomplete until we filmed the other side of the same conversation weeks later with Mr. Z, finally completing the scene. Performance wise do Actors like this? Not so much. Paycheck wise do Actors like this? Hail yeah!

PAGE COUNT

Another part of the checks and balances concerns page count, meaning 1) the total page count of the script, and 2) of each scene individually. As filming progresses, a daily tally is kept as to how many pages have been shot, and how many pages are owed. Studios try to gauge efficiency by how many pages are filmed in a day, or even by each part of the day. ADs assess how behind, on track, or ahead the shooting schedule is partially based on these numbers. TV or low-budget might average 5-7-10 pages on a normal day (whew), big budget shoots less. Much less.

Eighths – Each scene has a page count in 8^{ths}. A full page of scripted writing has eight eighths. A half page is shown as 4/8, never EVER ½, you math geeks out there. The page count, meaning the actual size of the scene or sum of all scenes, is different from the page number that appears at the top of each sheet of paper.

Page Count Per Page– It's about the amount of written material, not how many pieces of paper. The last page of a script may be numbered 100 in the upper right corner, but with revisions or, in episodic TV, Act breaks, some of those may be partial pages, having just a few lines on them. And with revisions, as scenes are shortened or lengthened, additional complete or partial pages may be tucked into the script.

More on Revisions in a moment, but briefly, similar to the added scenes, added revised pages would tuck in with the Dewey-ish decimalish system, but here with the **letter** added **AFTER the page number**. For example, as 1, 1A, 1B, 2, 3, 3A, 4, 5, with the letter after the number. Added page numbers **proceed**. Although this example shows pages 1 through 5, its actually 8 pieces of paper. And when things really get coo-coo in rewrites and omit-ting scenes, pages may even be "combined" and condensed. The number in the corner of the script page may show as 2-4.

We are interested in the amount of PRINT on the pages, not the number in the corner. For me, this is a quick handwritten exercise. I make a list of each page NUMBER in the script (the number in the corner), then next to each page number put the page COUNT (the amount of print on that page) in 8ths. Add each of those individual page counts together and viola we have the TOTAL PAGE COUNT.

Again the total page count is usually not the same as the last upper right page number of the script.

PAGE COUNT PER SCENE

Each *scene* has a count determined in eighths. A scene can be pages long, say 4 5/8, or a short 1/8 of a page. There aren't really rules as to so many lines of print = so much of a page count. I do it by eye. Or by button if using a digital Script Supervising program.

1/8 2/8 3/8 4/8 5/8 6/8 7/8 1 1 1/8 1 2/8 1 3/8 (get it?)

Beside each Scene number on the breakdown is listed its length in eighths of a page. And when each scene's length is added together the sum equals the Total Page Count for the whole script.

Doing a separate count by pages and by scenes provides a way to check that the totals match. And if they don't, check the numbers again for mathematical, human or computer formatting errors. And if the numbers still don't add up its time to go over each scene again.

To double check the Total Page Count of the script, the sum from the individual pages (not the number of sheets of paper but the amount of writing on each sheet) must equal the sum from the scenes. At wrap, the script's Total Page Count is the baseline to catch errors, meaning **total pages shot + total pages owed = the Total Page Count.**

"BUT-BUT-BUT-I'M-NOT-CONFUSED-ENOUGH-YET" ASIDE

Each page broken into 8th's mean there can only be 8 scenes per page. But WHAT IF the Writer has 10, 11, 12 small scenes on a page? They're using a mushy writing program! Low budget? I have only seen this once, and several of the scenes should've been clumped into a montage. A **montage** sequence can have quick pops of different images, from different locations even, lumped together forming an idea or relaying particular information, all in one paragraph. Pretty sneaky, eh?

Well, we deal with what we are given, if someone puts 12/8[th]s on a page (meaning 12 scene headings with a brief description), it may be better to reflect that. But rule of Thumbelina, a full page is only 8/8ths.

DAY / NIGHT

The information from the DAY/NIGHT breakdown folds into the master breakdown, shown with each scene.

Even if a story takes place over years, to clarify it is a new point in time with potential changes, we label scenes Day 1, 2, 3.... Possibly with a note in the description that it's a particular year or era in the story.

If the story unfolds chronologically there's technically no flashing back. If the film travels down memory lane, or if a scene pops back to show information from before the present time bubble of the main story, think flashback.

INTERIOR/EXTERIOR

Scenes are marked Interior or Exterior to clarify locations and lighting. If a scene is set in an Exterior park at night where a character is really wandering about the park, you film it at night. If a scene is set for an Interior bedroom at night, there are ways to light (or block light) to film by real life day. And vice versa. *

A scene can also be both INT/EXT, like filming from inside as well as outside of a car, or having a conversation take place in the front doorway with one character in the house and one character on the porch.

*Movies used to record "Day for Night," manipulating the film's exposure and the way the film would be processed to odd effect that would strangely work, enough. In older films notice how often exterior night scenes have clouds and shadows! This method would not fly with digital.

LOCATION

Follow the scene headings. Often a location will be shot out, so scenes that take place in the PARKING GARAGE, even if they have little to do with one another, will probably be shot on the same day. Each time Production has to move all of the equipment trucks and trailers, Extras' tents and catering tents, it costs time and money.

DESCRIPTION

Briefly and clearly relay what the scene is about, making sure to include characters, special props or actions. This is a quick reference for other departments as well as yourself.

TIME

It's handy to know what time of day a scene occurs to light accordingly, and also fill in blanks to track the day - do the kids enter the house wearing backpacks from school? Is dinner on the stove in the background? Should the hero car be at work and not in the driveway? Also, in case the film frame shows a watch or clock that must be set, or a calendar, it's good to be prepared, know where we are in the story timeline.

And for our DP and Electrician friends, lighting for 9:00 am looks different than lighting for 1:00pm. Speaking of time...

TIMING

The act of timing serves as a tool to estimate the duration of a script as a completed shot and edited movie. Television shows need a specific amount of content to place credits and commercials around, generally 22 or 45 minutes. Many features try to hover around 90 minutes, but of course have more room to grow. Why film more than you can use? From the Producer's standpoint, a Timing may be requested right off the bat.

Folks kick around this idea that a script will run about a minute a page. In theory, a 100 page script should run 100 minutes. The "standard." Meh, not so much. Honestly timing seems a little hit or miss, so much being dependent on the style of the Director and Actors and Editor. Gone with the Wind, "Atlanta burns," at $1/8^{th}$ of a page - 10 seconds? No. That being said, it can be a means to determine if a film runs long before even picking up a camera.

So how do *I* do a Timing? Stop watch in hand, I make sure no one else is in the house, and I read the script. Out loud. And with *feeeeling*, confirming why I am indeed working *behind* the camera. Point being is to act it out in 3 dimensions. If the script says someone crosses the room, cross the room, if the script says someone gets in their car and drives off, pretend to open the car door, start the ignition, put it in gear and peel away. It's a little awkward and silly until the task at hand takes over.

Those dang Kung Fu scenes always get me worked up.

After years of practice I time it twice and average it. First timing is read straight through, second time is scene by scene. If it helps the project, great! If they ignore the info, and, say in TV, continue to write weekly scripts that are too long and way over what they will use, don't take it personally.

AND THE TOTAL IS...

At the end of the breakdown, tally the total Number of Scenes in the script (remember, OMITS do not count), the Total Page Count, and list the Timing if production has asked (and paid) for one.

Then at the end of each shooting day, balancing credits and debits, the daily tally of **scenes completed + scenes owed = the Total Number of Scenes**. The daily tally of **pages shot + pages owed = Total Page Count**.

SCRIPT REVISIONS

And now word about revisions...

Writers like to write, and often update or revise the script even while filming is in full swing. Sometimes only after seeing the dailies, after seeing how the story translates to the screen, through the given Actors or Director, does a Writer discover a way to make that story clearer, better. They might add dialogue, shift scenes around, or change locations. When the script has been locked, instead of renumbering existing scenes or pages, the revisions mark the changes, big or small, in a way that disrupts the script (which hundreds of people have been working off of) as little as possible.

An asterisk * in the margin indicates a change in that specific line on each revised page, to quickly identify where in the script and on the page there's something different. It might be dialogue, description, a name change, or even something in the screen heading. Do the changes require updating the breakdown?

Each revision is color coded, and when the office distributes the new paper pages they are (should be) literally printed on colored paper.

With email distribution, make sure to read the color version of the file, also typed at the top of the revision pages. When deep in the exhaustive trenches of episodic television, and several versions of several scripts are floating around, it's easy to get a little mixed up glancing at several revisions while living in the current shooting script.

For each change, two sets of revisions should be sent out from the Office - collated, meaning a full version of the updated script, and revised pages only, just the pages that reflect the changes. When scripts were on paper only, this made it easier to replace just the revised pages instead of starting from scratch (and losing or transferring notes) with a whole new printout of the script.

Here's the traditional color order of revisions:

White	original locked script
Blue	1st revision
Pink	2nd revision
Yellow	3rd revision
Green	4th revision
Goldenrod	5th revision
Buff	6th revision
Salmon	7th revision
Cherry	8th revision
Tan	9th revision
Grey	10th revision
Ivory	11th revision
Double white	12th revision... and etc...

I made a song to help myself remember the color order of revisions – "blue, pink, yellow and green/goldenrod, buff, salmon and cherry/tan, gray, ivory/then we start over again." It sings more songy than it reads! Colored paper is a quick way to find the revised pages in a white paper script, with digital not so much.

The top of each revised page will state the draft color. Sometimes a show won't climb the color ladder, after goldenrod they might go to double blue, so just be aware. I've also seen shows use unique colors past a point.

Lavender revisions anyone?

Same with page numbers. If changes are made on a script page, the number of that page does not change, but newly added pages, even if only partial pages with a few lines, will take a letter on the other side – page 1, 1A, 1B, 2, the idea being that you re-place as few of the original pages in the script as possible. With each revision that changes page count, scene number or number of scenes, Day or Night, location, or description, the breakdown needs to be updated. If a revision reflects dialogue changes, but doesn't affect the page count or the story, I hold off on sending out a new breakdown. But if there's a change in Character, props, actions, or anything in the scene heading, I revise and send out the updated breakdown.

◆ ◆ ◆

BACK TO THE PREP - MEETINGS

Weeks and months of Prep equal many different meetings. While breaking down the script, discrepancies may stand out that need some clarification, or questions concerning how the pieces of the puzzle fit, or not. If concerns are red flag urgent con-tact the AD, who has most likely already been in on hundreds of conversations and meetings with other grown ups. If he or she doesn't have an answer they can find one. I try to go through AD before reaching out to Director or Writer myself. An AD may know the answer, or add your questions to a list of other concerns they will present to the grown ups anyway.

Regular questions may be answered during the production or tone meetings. And if not, since the Heads of Departments are often gathered at that time, ask for clarification. Believe me I want to open my mouth at these things as little as possible! But by piping up with a concern or discrepancy that was overlooked, it can be addressed in the NOW, not in the LATER when the crew is standing around on set burning daylight, waiting for some special prop to be made, a major wardrobe change or an last minute call to the writer.

PERSONAL KIT

On Set - of course prepare the on set bag with supplies and such, and set up the forms. I am old school, I am old period! On set I use an iPad but still make my chicken scratch notes on paper with a 4 colored pen (changing colors between takes). Other basics are flashlights and spare batteries, my own headphones, and a stop watch. I am not, however, the on-set office supply.

And just in case, for back up, I like to have a hardcopy of the script with all the other parts of the paper notes system - binder, ruler, printed forms, just what I need to do the job if electronics fail.

Eliminating paper notes has actually added about 8 lbs to my kit, for there's also an external battery charger for the pad, and a weather-proof case. Strive to be able to go with the flow regardless of weather, access to power, location, day or night, as independently and streamlined as possible. Each department has their own duties and pressures, and I for one do not want to depend on anyone running an extension cord or camera cable for me, especially while they are trying to take care of their OWN job.

Back Up - Another bag stays in the car with back up supplies, rain gear that can be tossed into the on set bag, extra socks and shoes, a hat and a change of clothes are packed up too. May I also recommend water, snacks and, for those who use them, feminine hygiene products. Ever tell you about the time I was working on a football movie in the sweaty Texas summer sun when my birthright came shockingly early? And the seatbacks (and bottoms) of the director's chairs were off-white? Egad! Crisis averted by being prepared.

Because I work away from my hometown, just before blast off I also pack up what I can of an office for wherever I am staying – printer/scanner and photo-printer if needed, laptop and supplies. Better to have them and not use them than need them and not have them.

DESCRIBING THE SHOT

The Editor and Assistants work to put together the best parts of the footage to tell the strongest version of the story they can. Which means they have their own work world, and though they may visit, they are not on set. The Script Supervisor acts as eyes and ears, transcribing in several pages what and how we've shot over the course of the day, as well as reminding the Director to get all of the pieces needed for each scene to cut together.

Let's cover what goes in the notes, then how to organize them.

In describing the shot, potentially a hundred plus shots a day, we want to relay info clearly and concisely, making it as easy as possible to scan over our notes and find something in particular, for the editors as well as for self. We take in several streams of information for hours each day, and are tasked with imparting the key elements from each shot. Imagine concisely detailing what the image is to someone that isn't seeing the footage, in as few words as possible.

Every time a camera rolls there is a note to be taken.

IT'S A SET UP

Lights! Camera! Action! is sometimes, often, like:

Scene 17 is up. Blocking rehearsal, so cameras can see where the Actors will stand during the first take. OK, send Actors to get ready. Let's get to work!

Lights! Points (ladder or track) coming through, here comes a Grip with a stand, make way for the scissor lift so the

Electricians can adjust lights in the grid over the set, bring in a quarter CTO (gel)... While –

Camera! OK after the Grips finish setting up the dolly track we'll place the B camera there. Put A camera in hand held mode. Go to the truck to get that fish eye lens. When we can look at the shot we'll see if we need Art Department to dress something on that blank wall back there. I'ma get a sammich, you want anything? Until finally –

Action! Oh no wait, invite the Actors down from base camp, let's do a camera rehearsal, and mic up the Actors. "Last looks" for Wardrobe, H/MU, Props, and...and...

Aaaand Action!

Preparing to film a scene on the day can take a bit of work. And time. When all of the people and all of the gear are in place for a particular shot, we can roll, and this particular arrangement is called a **Set Up**. Cuz there's so much to set up! Each set up gets described on the **Script Page**, **Left Hand Page** and **Daily Shot List**. And at wrap all set ups are tallied on the **Daily Report**, then added to a running total of set ups, updated daily. More on these forms to come.

Each time the camera position or framing changes, making for a different looking shot within the same scene, it's considered a new set up, and the Slate number advances to reflect such.

SLATE

Slate - the noun and the verb. Our movie-loving culture is familiar with the slate or clapper, where the top-striped stick claps down on a handheld board displaying the filming information.

Striking the clapper for each camera was once a way to sync up the sound roll with the picture roll in editing. The sound of the clap on the audio tape was manually lined up with the film frame image where the striped sticks hit. Today syncing sound and picture relies on matching up the digital Timecode running on the slate with the Timecode data from the cameras and sound. The "clap" is a back up.

The slate is a visual and sound cue usually preceding the shot (but sometimes it gets tagged at the end as a Tail Slate). The Project, the Director, the Director of Photography and the date are on the slate all day. But the information of note is:

- what camera roll
- what scene/what set up is being filmed
- what take
- any special frame rate or VFX
- episode number for TV

Basically the **slate number is the scene number with the set up number.** Script Sup clarifies what this number is based on what's being filmed. The 2nd ACs will put this on the slate, then call out the set up and take number before hitting the sticks on each camera. The scene number, take and camera rolls are put in the notes.

Each time the camera rolls there should be a slate to correspond with the notes. Repeated attempts at the same camera angle and frame size become sequential **takes** (take 1,2,3,4...). If the Director wants the same but just part of the take it's slated as a **pick up** (take 5PU). If she just wants to run through something repeatedly without stopping it's on a **series** (take 6PU series – more below).

How does it work? The very first go at a scene, the first time filming anything starting anywhere in scene 17, the slate and notes reflect just that, 17, through each take. If Director gets what they need from the takes slated as number 17 then:

- the cameras change position, or framing, or
- the cameras change what character to follow, or
- we jump to a different part of scene 17

...whether there are lighting tweaks or not, it's on to a new set up which gets a new slate number by adding a letter. What wizardry is this? In this example, that's called 17A (adding letters of the alphabet instead of numbers but YES this is still called a slate *number*). So after slate 17 the next slate would be 17A, then 17B, then 17C and on after that.

What if?

IF both cameras have new shots, advance the slate to the next letter.

IF the main/A camera sets up for a new shot but the B camera stays the same, advance the slate to the next letter.

IF A cam stays the same but B camera changes in an important main camera sort of way, advance the slate to the next letter,

IF the A camera stays the same, but B cam will just be fishing around, go to the next TAKE number and note the change.

If we don't finish shooting out scene 17 and come back to it another day, the slate picks up at the next set up letter.

Advancing the Slate – Military call letters

Again, in slating we use letters not numbers to advance through the scene, or scene 17 set up 2 would look like 172, but what if there *is* a scene 172? We use the alphabet, except for the letters I and O, for they resemble the numbers 1 and 0. Some folks don't use letter U because it can look like a V. I do!

For clarity, when telling sound and camera the slate, instead of saying the letter, a word is used to represent the letter. The Military call signs are standard but using names or other objects is common too - Apple, Baker, Denver, Edward, Franklin, George, Kansas, Peter, Quincy, Thomas, Uncle...

The first set up for scene 17 is just the scene number – 17. The next set up is 17A, "Apple's up!" After that comes 17B, "Let's go to Baker." See the pattern? 17C, "Seventeen Charlie!"

MILITARY ALPHABET

A — Alpha	N — November
B — Bravo	(O h no you didn't)
C — Charlie	P — Papa
D — Delta	Q — Quebec
E — Echo	R — Romeo
F — Foxtrot	S — Sierra
G — Golf	T — Tango
H — Hotel	U — Uniform
(I is not for you)	V — Victor
J — Juliet	W — Whiskey (please)
K — Kilo	X — X-ray
L — Lima	Y — Yankee
M — Mike	Z — Zulu

With a big and detailed scene, slates can easily get to 17Z.

Then? Then start over, with "A" locked in after the scene number, as in 17AA, 17AB, 17AC...17AZ. Then? 17BA, 17BB, 17BC...it
happens.

When does a slate not reflect a scene number? Sometimes a
script will break up continuous action, intercutting scenes from
another location. So the action of scene 17 may run continuously
into scenes 19 and 21, but would be slated with the scene number
where the shot begins. The script pages would be lined through
each scene filmed accordingly, with a squiggle through the interim scenes (18 and 20) if short, or an indicator guiding the Editor to page X or to scene 19 if the interim scenes are pages long.

SPECIALTY SLATES

Also, occasionally a Director wants to catch something
generic on the fly, like a sunset, or a hero car parked in front of the
hero house, for a potential transition without knowing where he
will cut it into the film. Thus this could be slated SUNSET or CAR
or XX or INSERT.

MOS

Often inserts don't roll sound. These shots are **MOS** – Minus
Optical Stripe* (NOT Mitt Out Sound, don't let anyone fool ya).
When slating, the clapper stays closed or a hand blocks the sticks,
reminding the Editor the take is MOS, and to keep them from fran-
tically searching for the missing soundtrack.

*Back when film was on celluloid, the soundtrack was a zig
zaggy stripe on the actual film strip, to the right of the frames in
lieu of that one side of sprocket holes.

Wildlines

Speaking of sound/no sound, sometimes a script has a section of speech meant to be heard, not seen, like narration, or even

a voice over the telephone. If this is recorded on set, only sounds rolls, and the camera stands down. The Sound Mixer names the sound slate "Wildline scene 45" and it goes in the notes as such.

Wildsound

As above to capture ambient sound, Roomtone, or Wala - crowd chatter.

World Series

If no sound is needed to roll on some small shot, or there's a little piece of the scene the Director wants to quickly film *several* takes of in a single take, that's on a **SERIES**. For example an insert shot of a hand lifting an envelope up into frame so the viewer can see the address. Instead of cutting the camera, reslating and doing another take, on a series the Actor would just repeat the action, lifting the envelope into frame, several times in a row with whatever variations the Director asks for. If there's no cut, sound stays in sync. If there's no need to record sound, there's no sync that cuts could effect. This would be slated as the next set up number series – "17C series."

Tail Slate

If cameras had to roll without a slate, or there was a total misslate, there is a chance for redemption – the Tail Slate! This basically is a slate at the end of the shot. After the Director calls "cut" cameras keep rolling to pop the slate in, upside down as a visual cue that the slate's at the end of what was just shot.

X Marks The Spot

A small crew filming separately from the main unit is called 2nd Unit. Sometimes there's no sound, there might be a Producer calling the shots, there may be Stand-Ins or stunt doubles instead of the Actors. 2nd Unit often picks up inserty bits or shots missed when the main unit filmed the scene. Here the slate starts with the scene number, preceded with an X – X17, X17A, X17B...

TV shows will sometimes overlap episodes, and though it may be called 2nd Unit the work is actually additional main unit work, with the Actors and Director filming full scenes. This would be slated as normal, no preceding X. Unless main unit Script Sup needs something different.

Viva La V

When green screen is in the shot or there's another visual effect that will have to be computer generated in post, it's handy to put a V in front of the slate number, again for quick identification (V17D). Sometimes a Visual Effects Person will be present, sometimes it's up to us to remember. VFX may also need certain measurements in the notes from camera, as depth, height, distance and settings.

Sometimes VFX needs a **PLATE SHOT,** a static shot of the location. This can be slated as the next take number with notation, given a new set up or called something like 17 Plate.

R U Ready For The Last One?

After viewing the dailies, if a set up, say 17A, needs to be reshot, needs to match exactly what was filmed the first time only more better, an R precedes the set up number- R17A.

R U Ready For The Last Last One? Commercials

Slating on commercials is different. Often the scripts aren't scripts. They might be boards (drawings) or a few paragraphs of description, or different commercial spots. There aren't scene numbers per se. Usually set up numbers run sequential starting with 101, 102, 103... The second day of filming can carry on or start 201, 202, 203.... Not so much with the Apple, Baker. Sometimes there's no sound, sometimes the situation won't allow the AC to pop in a slate, so the notes alone may indicate when camera changes are made.

OK back to our Action!

Flip ahead to the example of Scene 86, take 1. Here, two cameras film the same action but with differing results – the A camera is hand held and the B camera is a smooth dolly move.

Two cameras rolling during the same take is counted as two set ups.

Same Slate number, same take number but different shots. A Slate number can have multiple takes - all the takes should be similar as far as the camera movement and framing is concerned. With exceptions mentioned above.

A Slate number or set up doesn't have to cover the whole scene, or even start from the beginning of a scene. A set up can show all the characters for the whole scene, or just a line of dialogue from one character, or just an insert shot of an object.

A simple way to quickly relay who or what is being filmed for what parts of the scene is by lining the script page.

LINING (AND SQUIGGLING) THE SCRIPT

As a quick visual reference for the Editor, each camera's set up (not each take) is marked on the script with a vertical line running down the page over the section of the scene being shot in that set up. **Each vertical line represents a Slate and it's camera set up – two cameras, two set ups, two vertical lines.** A Slate can cover pages, a single word of dialogue, a reaction, an action, or an object. Slate number scene number 86...

A straight line indicates what's seen on camera for that set up, and a squiggle marks what was not filmed or is off screen. At a glance the Editor can see the Slate number and what dialogue or action is shown on camera in each set up.

Next slate number, 86A. Camera A might be on MADDY and Camera B on LAUREL. On the script page, the slate number "86A" is written where the set up begins in the scene, and beneath it a vertical line is drawn for each camera rolling. On Camera A's vertical line, we keep every bit of Maddy's dialogue said on camera straight, and over Laurel's dialogue we make a squiggle (since she is not seen speaking on Camera A's shot). And vice versa for Camera B – Laurel's dialogue, on screen, will have a straight line on the script page, and Maddy's part of the dialogue, off screen, will have a squiggle.

Slate numbers and the corresponding notes, takes and times are written on the Left Hand Page and the Daily Shot List.

◆ ◆ ◆

NOTES ABOUT NOTES

TIME

From "action" to "cut" each take is timed and noted. Sometimes the Director will ask how long the takes are averaging, ACs might ask as well to assess whether they can squeeze another take on the camera roll/memory card before a reload. Timing the rehearsals can be a help in this as well.

Using the Master Shot, which runs through the whole scene, a take may last 2 minutes. With all those unnecessary dramatic pauses, slow looks and fumbles taken out, the scene when edited may only be 1 minute and a half. This "how it should be edited" time is put on the report for the estimated time a scene runs.

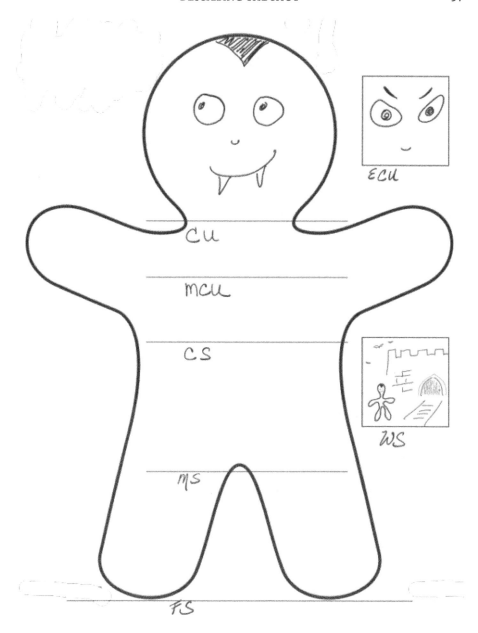

FRAME SIZES

Often several sizes and perhaps angles of the same action are filmed and edited together to build up tension or show emotion. This is called **coverage** - we cover the scene with different sized shots or different angles to edit together.

Frame size is a storytelling tool. It's also mighty big delineator in noting the shots. How much of a person, place or thing fills the frame?

LS – **long shot** – an extremely wide shot, people look small on the screen in the context of the landscape

WS – **wide shot** – still wide, like an establishing shot of a house. People still have some open frame around their bodies

FS – **full shot** – vampires are basically framed head to toe

MS – **medium shot** – cuts off at the hip area

CS – **close shot** – from the chest

MCU – **medium close up** – beneath the shoulders

CU – **close up** – the head

ECU – **extreme close up** – just the face, or the mouth, or eyes...

SUBJECT

The frame size corresponds with the subject of the shot. Noting the on-camera character is a necessary part of the notes.

> MS Cindy - Medium shot of Cindy, this means from hips or waist up.

If several characters are on camera it helps to write them in order from **frame left to frame right.**

> MS Cindy and Bobby – Medium shot, Cindy and Bobby from the waist up, also known as ...
>
> M2S Cindy and Bobby - Medium Two Shot Cindy and Bobby from the waist up.

How about this...

> 4S Cindy, Bobby, Jan and Peter – Four Shot Cindy, Bobby, Jan and Peter, with no specific frame size.

The subject can also be a place, or a thing.

> CU glove – Close Up on a glove.

> WS Pond – Wide Shot of a pond.

ANGLES

Is the camera placed noticeably above or below the subject?

HA – **high angle** – The camera is placed high, looking down on the subject

LA – **low angle** – The camera is placed low, looking up at the subject

CANTED or **DUTCH** angle – Like the old Batman Show, the camera is askew.

In contemporary filmmaking anything goes for style or to change it up. In film's history, often the camera looking up at a character implied they were dominant, and looking down on a character meant they were weak.

CAMERA MOVEMENT

Camera movement adds energy to a shot and can be a storytelling tool. A shaky camera feels different from a super slick crane move. A pan of the camera can reveal new information to the viewer. Some shows always have the camera on a dolly, slowly creeping back and forth just enough to subtly distract from the bad acting. Kidding!

Dolly or Tracking Shot – camera's on a dolly (a cart, you know, with wheels) moving forward towards or backwards from the subject, or following along side, parallel. The dolly can also be set on rails or track.

HH – Handheld – the camera is held by the Operator – on the shoulder, or on a camera rig that hangs on the Operator's body.

Steadicam – camera's mounted to a calibrated stabilization rig worn by the Steadicam Operator that isolates the Op's movements from the camera for a smoother shot. The steadicam can "push" meaning walking behind the subject or "pull," walking backwards, in front of the subject, track parallel, walk circles around a subject, almost anything if the space allows.

Pan – the camera pivots from left to right (or right to left), on an axis like shaking your head "no." Think of filming a tennis match from the net line.

Tilt – the camera pivots up to down (or down to up), on an axis like nodding your head "yes." Think of filming a glass elevator going up from a courtyard lobby.

Crane – the camera's mounted on a weighted arm or pole (boom) so it moves on a greater arc, like being on one end of a giant see saw, except this can move camera up and down and side to side and in between fluidly! Some cranes lift the Camera Operator with the camera, some cameras are worked remotely. Some are mounted on a special dolly, and some are so massive they are mounted on their own truck! Swoop the day away.

Jib – Son of Crane, much smaller, may be mounted on a regular camera dolly.

Aerial Shot /Drone Shot – as it sounds, taken from the air.

OVERS

Overhead – can be tied back to the crane and jib, camera is over, aimed down onto the scene.

OTS – **Over the Shoulder** – in filming a conversation this creates intimacy within context. The shot may be on Cindy, but catches a piece of Bobby between her and the camera, to help the viewer feel she is speaking to Bobby.

> Cindy OTS L – Cindy Over the Left Shoulder, over Bobby's left shoulder, so Cindy's face is on the left side of the frame, and Bobby (his back) is on the right side of frame.

When it's time to shoot the reverse, Bobby speaking to Cindy, camera goes over her RIGHT shoulder. This will (hopefully) magically make more sense in a moment, but think about basics, like Pong level basics. Bobby is always on the right side of frame, be it his face or just the back of his shoulder, and Cindy is always on the left side of the frame.

French Overs – sometimes used when people are side by side, like on a park bench or couch. This is like an over-over, from behind both of the Actors, like camera sitting in the backseat of a car with the Actors in the front, camera going over the inside shoulders rather than the outside shoulders.

SCREEN DIRECTION

Is there an action by camera or an Actor that moves in a particular direction? A camera pans left, an Actor walks off frame right…this info can relate to geographical space, or be the basis for matching movement in another shot.

More will be revealed on overs and screen direction, they

are tied to "the line."

SPECIALTY SHOTS

Well, maybe not *that* special, these shots or techniques are used often. Believe me, we've seen these our whole movie and television viewing life!

EST – **Establishing shot** - These are about location and thus tend to be wide, serving as a way to let the audience know where the story is about to go. In editing, an establishing shot of the Empire State building that cuts to an office scene implies that office is in the Empire State building.

Insert Shot – At best, a pop of something the Director wants the audience to really notice that adds a lil something to the story. It could be a close up of an Actor's interaction with an object, as a cell phone in hand, the writing on a document, a photograph, or a reveal for the viewer. Think of all those action movies where unbeknownst to the hero a time bomb is ticking away beneath the desk. Unbeknownst to the hero, but shown to the audience. At not so best, an insert shot is used to cover up a clumsy cut in editing!

Sometimes inserts are "cheated," for example using a Stand-In's hand wearing the same ring and watch as the Actor's character.

Master Shot – This is typically a wider shot of a scene run from start to finish that establishes action. In editing, a scene may begin and end in the Master. On set, when an Actor stands up on a certain line in the wide Master, they should stand up at the same point when in Medium Shot and Close Up.

Ideally Masters are filmed first to establish action and kind of warm everyone up for all those beautiful Close-Ups. Occasionally the Master will be filmed toward the end of filming the scene. One reason is an Actor that loses their freshness with repetition and thus for performance it's better to get the closer shots first.

One-er - If there's only one set up of a scene, and thus the only option, it's called a One-er. One set up. There's no action or look lines within the scene that have to match in a closer shot because there is no closer shot. One and done.

POV – **Point of View** – Here the camera acts as a character's eyes and reveals what specifically they are seeing, be it the desk in front of them, or another person.

Rack – The focus of the lens intentionally shifts between planes of focus, like foreground and background subjects.

Raking shot – a staggered profile. Picture 3 faces in profile, in a row, from a slight angle so the faces overlap from foreground to background.

Got all that? So a note for the Editor may look like this:

HA dolly to CS Cindy OTS R – meaning high angle dolly into a close shot of Cindy over the right shoulder (of Bobby).

EST House sunset – is just that, an Establishing shot of the house at sunset.

M2S Cindy and Bobby rack CU Dog – Medium 2 shot Cindy and Bobby, rack focus to Close Up of Dog in Foreground.

POV pan R Car - Point of View shows car, camera pans right.

Daily Shot List

Title: _BFF_   Date: _4-10-20_
Director: _Beatrice Alexander_   Day: _7 of 21_
Script Supervisor: _Sheila Strabley_   Page: _3 of_

Slate	Scene	Camera/Sound Rolls	Prints	Time	Description
84A	84, 85	A21/S7	1	52	A M2S Laurel Maddy
		B/S	2 inc	17	B MCU Laurel
			3	47	
			(4)	50	
84B	84, 85	A21/S7	(1)	45	steadicam 2S
85	85	A21/S7	1	25	E+A crane girls
~~tails~~			2	30	enter cemetery
			(3)	27	
85A	85	A21/S7	1	15	A insert tomb candle
		B/S	(2) ser	41	B feet
86	86	A21/S7	1	33	A HH sign to M2S
		B/S	2	35	B dolly F2S
		A22	(3)	31	
			(4) ✕	33	
86A	86	A22/S7	1	27	A MCU Maddy OTS
		B/S	(2)	30	B MCU Laurel OTS
			(3)	35	
86B	86	B/S/—	(1)	12	LA POV sign

Script Page: 38
Date: 4-10-20

Crane   14

Slate	CR	SR	Take/ Time		Comments	Description	Lens
85	A21	S7	1	25	Stacked	EHA WS boom &
tail! stix			2	30	bumpy	Maddy Laurel cemetary
			③	27		
85A						inserts
	A21	S7	1	15	candle out	A rack tomb to candle
	B15		②	41	② slower step	B CS feet
					-3 laurel first	
86					exit L	HH, dolly
	A21	S7	1	33	too big	A Handheld tilt sign
	B15		2	35	/me 1 "bread"	to MaS
	[A22		③	31		B dolly F2S Maddy Laurel
		*	④	33	good wiping	
86A						overs
	A22	S7	1	27		A MCU Maddy OTS L
	B15		②	30		B MCU Laurel OTS Rt
			③	35		
86B						POV
	B15	—	①	12		LA Sign

38.

(84) (84A) (84B)   LAUREL
                                 (singing)
                            It's my pity party and I'll cry if
                            I want to. (stops joking) We live
                            on a trauma planet. But maybe
                            there's enough beauty here to make
                            it worthwhile.

85   EXT. CEMETERY - NIGHT   85
              (85) (85A)
          They reach the corner. An old cemetery glows, a candle lit at
          each grave. No one's about. They step over the low concrete
          wall and wander into the calm strange beauty of it.

                                              FADE OUT.

86   EXT. FRENCH QUARTER STREET - NIGHT   86
                     (86)   (86B)
          Candlelight is replaced by neon and gas lamps as they near
          the heart of the Quarter. More music. Maddy notices a
          restaurant sign.

                            MADDY   (86A)
                       Ooo, po'boys, can you eat that? Bet
                       they can do just cheese.   bread

                            LAUREL
                       Maybe there's a baked potato or
                       something.

                            MADDY
                         (good god, it's the booze
                          talking)
                       Aaaah, ooo, fried oysters, yeah
                       lets go there.

87   EXT. FRENCH QUARTER ALLEY - NIGHT   87

          LATER

          A husband and wife DUO perform their music in the street.
          Nearby Laurel holds Maddy's hair and feathers back while she
          pukes in the alley. Ridiculous.

                            MADDY
                         (gasping)
                       It wasn't (urp) the oysters
                       (heave). I think it was the (urp)
                       sauce.

FORMS AND ORGANIZING NOTES FOR THE EDITOR

There's a basic Script Supervisor protocol used for relaying and organizing the information gleaned from each take, whether utilizing a pre-made program or creating forms for taking on-set notes. With practice, forms can be adjusted to fit with each person's developing workflow, or can be adapted to a particular project's needs.

At the day's end, copies of these notes are sent to the Office, Editorial and ADs. These notes are a map of sorts, bursting with information when you understand the codes and clues.

BASIC FORMS
Daily Progress Report
Daily Shot List
Left Hand Page
Lined Script Page
Lunch Report
Wardrobe Outline
Owed List

A PYRAMID OF NOTES, FROM TOP TO BOTTOM
Whether using paper or computer, each filming day the Script Sup organizes levels of information on several forms, compress-

ing detail from each day's script notes up to the **DAILY PROGRESS REPORT**. For each day this top sheet reflects:

- scenes completed
- scenes only partially shot
- "edited" minutes and seconds completed for each scene or part
- wild lines
- camera and sound rolls
- the day's tally, and a running show tally, of scenes completed, pages shot, number of set ups and an estimate of how many edited minutes were shot
- clock times, as first shot, lunch and camera wrap
- any important side notes

This is the last form to get filled out. At the end of each filming day a copy of the Daily Progress Report, the top sheet, goes to the ADs.

More details are revealed with the **DAILY SHOT LIST,** posting in the order in which each set up was filmed (thus in order of how the clips will appear on the camera rolls):

- each slate/set up
- scene(s) correlating to each slate
- camera and sound roles, with reloads
- takes and timings of shots
- circle takes
- brief description of the shot, for each camera

It's easier to skim through a couple of Shot List pages instead of flipping through the whole script and each scene. At a glance one can find what camera roll has that Close Up of Susie Q, that POV of the record player, or see there are 6 takes of 17D, with the B Camera reloading for take 3.

A copy of the in-progress Daily Shot List also goes to Editorial or Post with the lunchtime film break. Circle takes are marked and noted by the Post Production folks as they log in the notes to match up the footage. (Circle takes are also marked on the Left Hand Page and the camera reports.)

IN TO THE SCRIPT

Working scripts are printed on one side of the paper only. Imagine a paper script is open flat on your lap. The left piece of paper would be blank (backside of the previous page) and the right paper would have a scene printed on it. It's the terrain and we create a map of information with it.

For quick reference as to where or what line in the scene something of note occurs, **number each chunk of dialogue**. Some folks number each actual line of type in each scene, but for me numbering each section of dialogue has sufficed.

Here we also **LINE THE SCRIPT PAGE** as a quick visual reference of each slate number and set up, marking the scene coverage of each set up, and who and what is shot, as previously explained.

The Script Sup lines the script page, and puts notes on the "blank" page, on the left hand side of the open script, across from the script page where the particular slate/set up begins in the scene.

Line the script on the right, take notes on the left. In the paper example, the **LEFT HAND PAGE** can be on the blank backside of the script or can be a separate form inserted in the script. What kind of notes? Well, what information would help Editorial locate and identify a particular shot out of hundreds of hours of footage?

-    the date

- the slate number
- camera and sound rolls
- the takes and their times
- a brief description of each set up on each camera
- circle takes, mis-slates, errors during the take
- lens setting

SLATING IN THE TRENCHES

Script Supervisor calls out the slate number for Camera and Sound to mark the shot identically. When filming moves fast and folks get exhausted, communication can get mushy. If there's a booboo don't call any person out, just notate and try to correct it for the next time. Try not to yell the person's name across a quiet rolling set to correct a slate! If it feels appropriate politely call the take number out again, address the slater as their position as in B Camera or Sound, ask DIT to tell them over their walkie channel or ask for a tail slate but don't call anyone out personally! Would you want the spotlight on you if (lets be honest, WHEN) you make a mistake?

If the set is not in frantic filming mode and it feels OK to call out the correction without making a big deal try, "It's take 4" or then "B cam take 4" if they aren't hearing you, never "Hey Donut Face, it's take 4!" Maybe they didn't hear you, or maybe you didn't make yourself heard, be kind.

Sometimes the slates roll before you get back to the monitors, but if possible it's good to see them to make sure they are correct. If the slate is wrong ask for a tail slate or note the error and correct the 2nd AC for the next take.

Respect the 2nd ACs, they can give us a heads up of the frame rate is changing, if camera ended up with new orders while we were helping an Actor and they may overhear information before we do. They let us know when there's a reload, which goes in the notes. Share and help them and they can share and help you.

Reloading means the 2nd AC will start a new camera report, and before the day is done Script Sup marks the preferred or circle takes on all the camera reports. Some shows want the sound report circled too. Return these reports to Camera/Sound to go to Editorial with their rolls.

LUNCH REPORT

The Big Cheese at the Studio wants to know how the shooting day's going (how the money's being spent), so at lunch the Script Sup tallies the number of set ups, pages shot, minutes shot and scenes, completed or partial, for the first part of the day. The invested Producers want to see what time the first shot got off. By recording this information, the Script Sup is a witness in a way.

WARDROBE OUTLINE

The Wardrobe Department keeps detailed track of each character's clothing for each scene, making a tome of their own. But things change, lines of communication get crossed, an Actor plays with his stuff, the Costumer in-the-know isn't the one on set that day, on and on. Thus it's of great help to have the basics jotted down for a double-check with a continuity picture. Jewelry placement, clothing description and colors, sleeves rolled, top button undone, shirt tucked, backpack, sunglasses and such can easily accidentally end up askew otherwise.

OWED LIST

Those dangling shots owed when a scene is mostly complete should be noted on the DPR so the ADs remember to schedule them in. These can be wish list shots, or pieces necessary to complete the scene, be at an insert or something with an Actor. Then keep a running list or a form for self, and be aware of any opportunities to knock any of those shots out.

CAMERA: TO BE SMARTER THAN THE AVERAGE BEAR, KEEP READING

A Quick Note About Lenses

My husband says that a camera is basically a box with a lens attached. In essence that's true.

For matching sizes or reshoots, and often for special VFX shots, it's good for Script Sup and ACs to note the lens setting for each set up. But now with digital the information's in the metadata (oo lala). Also the setting may change during a shot as zoom lenses seem to be used more, at least in this neck of the woods.

The end.

But wait there's more! Much more, like what lenses do.

For this purpose the lens is the whole barrel or housing that gets mounted on the camera, not just one piece of glass. A good lens can cost more than the camera! The barrel holds lenses, pieces of curved glass, called **elements**. The elements and the distance between them effect magnification.

Light enters the lens. Passing through the curved glass causes the light rays to bend and converge or cross. This spot has the sharpest focus – the **focal point**. The distance between this point and the digital sensor (or film gate with physical film) in the camera is the **focal length**. This distance is expressed numerically in millimeters and describes or "names" the lens. A 10 mm lens is shorter than a 200mm lens. The human eye sees at around

30-50mm.

A physically short lens captures a wider shot, and a longer lens, often with more glass (think like a telescope) creates more magnification making the subject appear closer. A shorter lens makes the subject look further, a longer lens makes it look closer, even telephoto.

Here's a rough example: You are standing in front of a house with a camera. Through a **Wide 10mm lens** the camera frame fills with the house, the grass in front, the trees on the side, sky over the house.

Your natural eye view, **Standard 35-50mm**, basically sees the facade of the house, (a lens mm below that range would be wide, beyond that would be long).

Through a **Long 135mm lens** only the front door fills the frame.

Lens choices affect storytelling by guiding the viewer's eyes to different types of information.

- **Wide Angle Lens** – wide shots, lower mm number, shorter barrel
- **Standard Lens** – midrange mm, closer to what the human eye sees
- **Long Lens** – for getting closer, telephoto, higher mm number, longer barrel
- **Prime lens** - has one fixed focal length - a 55 mm lens is just that
- **Zoom lens** - structurally more complicated, the focal length can be adjusted within a set range, so a single lens can range from 70-200mm, for example

APERTURE and F-STOPS and I. S. O.H MY

And how the lenses work, if you're curious...

There's an **Aperture**, an opening that controls the amount of light that enters the lens. An **Iris** expands and contracts the aperture, like the pupil in the human eye.

Think of filming by birthday cake, covered in candles. The room would be dark, so we'd open up the aperture all the way to let in as much available light as possible.

"...Happy Birthday to yooooouuuu..."

The candles are blown out and then the bright overhead lights are turned on. "My eyes!" Now too much light comes into the wide-open aperture, so we dial down - click click click - to a smaller opening. With each click down the aperture hole closes, gets smaller, letting in half as much light in from the previous click or setting. Closing the aperture is squeezing down or stopping more light (too much light) from reaching the sensor. Like squinting on a sunny day.

When the DP says "Stop it down" or "Open it up" the Camera crew adjusts the aperture setting on the camera.

Ready for more specifics?

The Aperture is adjustable by increments called f/**stops**. The f/stop is the ratio of the **focal length** (the distance from the image sensor to the focal point in the lens - where the light rays cross) to the **diameter** of the aperture (size of the opening). So the millimeter of lens over the size of the opening.

Have an old still camera kicking around the house? Notice a band of numbers on the lens – f/1.4, 2, 2.8, 4, 5.8, 8, 11, 16, up to f/22. Looking into the front of the lens, when set at f/2 the aperture would be rather wide open. Click it down to f/22 and the iris will fan in leaving only a small opening.

Each click down represents a half of the light transmitted from the previous f/stop. Remember these are ratios, **fractions**, so f/2 is **bigger** than f/22. Using fractions, 1/2 of that birthday cake is a bigger slice than 1/22. Chocolate, by the way.

A **larger aperture (opening) means a larger f/stop number**. In theory there's less available light or less 'candles' so the aperture is opened up. ...f/1.4, f/2, f/2.8...

A **smaller aperture (opening) means a smaller f/stop number**. In theory there's more light or more 'candles' so the aperture is closed down. ...f/11, f/16, f/22...

OK, so?

So? Sew a button on your underwear. The f/stop, meaning size of the aperture, affects what's in focus in the image. More precisely the Depth of Field.

DEPTH OF FIELD

Understanding focus...

The Depth of Field isn't in the camera or the lens, its "out there," a set distance from the camera. Think of a stationary bubble of focus in the landscape. A small bubble will have very little in focus, a larger bubble will have more. Now think of the bubble as an invisible rectangular box, in 3D. Only what is within the dimensions of that box is in focus. Now stretch that and think of it as a dimensional plane, and ONLY what is within that plane is in focus. This is the **focal plane**.

Good grief what am I talking about?

Another poor example, with made up parameters: We are filming Little Jimmy sitting on the beach about 10 feet away from the camera.

At $f/2$, an f-stop where the aperture or opening is wide, the depth of field (the plane or box of focus) would be **shallow**. Only things that are 10 feet to 10 ½ feet away from the camera would be in focus. Only objects within those wee wee 6 inches (the **focal plane**) between 10 feet and 10 ½ feet away would be in focus, say Jimmy's face. If Jimmy leans forward beyond those 6 inches his face will go out of focus.

At $f/8$ the aperture is smaller, closed down quite a bit, so the focal plane is deeper. Like how squinting helps further objects come into focus. Now everything between 9 feet and 12 feet away from the camera is in focus - Jimmy's whole body, the pail of sand at his side, the dog sleeping at his back. Here the focal plane is 3 feet deep.

At $f/22$ the aperture opening is quite small, which means the focal plane is *even* deeper, so everything from 6 feet to 25 feet from the camera is in focus – Jimmy, pail and dog, sand and the waves in the water behind them.

Sometimes the amount of available light dictates the $f/$ stop and depth of field, but sometimes it's an artistic choice. Selective focus is a story telling tool that controls the visual information shown, and guide the viewer's eye.

ISO - LIGHT SENSITIVITY

Let there be light!

Motion picture and still photography film stock is rated for **light sensitivity**. Celluloid is covered with an emulsion of silver halide particles. Smaller particles mean more particles can fit on the frame, resulting in a refined, sharp image. But these small particles can only do their best thing with a lot of light. This type of film stock is not as sensitive to low light and will have a lower EI

(Exposure Index) number.

A higher EI means more light sensitivity, means the film stock will do better in a low light situation, but at a cost – the silver halide particles are bigger, sometimes so big you can actually see them. This is the grain. Like the difference in wheat – powdery refined bleached pastry flour vs. a hearty stone-milled cracked wheat.

With digital we aren't swapping out memory cards that are more or less sensitive to light. The camera, or the sensor chip, has a set range of sensitivity, now referred to as **ISO** (International Standards Organization), which can be selected. With hi-falootin-tech, grain has become less of an issue, and often more of an effect.

FRAME RATE

A need for speed! Or not.

A lot can be done digitally in post, but often the Director will manipulate the speed of the image in camera, for all that dramatic slow motion.

The Frame rate is the speed, at so many frames per second (**fps**) that the film runs through the camera – or in digital terms, the speed at which the camera is set to record.

Be it film or video, the same principles apply, compared to the standard frame rate.

The faster the camera records, the slower the motion appears in playback.
The slower the camera records, the faster the motion appears in playback.

The altered frame rate should be noted on the slate and on the Left Hand Page. Also, Sound does not change the speed at which they record – this is all about the camera. The sound won't sync up with a faster or slower image, so sometimes Sound will stand down during an altered frame rate take.

In film the standard rate is 24 fps. In digital the standard is considered 30fps, well almost.

If you understand enough you may want to skip ahead, otherwise read on at your own risk of further confusion.

FILM

Theaters (remember those?) project the film at a rate that replicates how our eyes see in nature. The standard rate projected on the big screen, "tricking" our eyes to make all these individual pictures or still frames appear to run together in smooth motion, is **24 fps**. This occurs via a sort of visual memory, called Persistence of Vision.

To replicate human vision and smooth natural motion, cameras film at 24 fps and theaters project film at 24 fps.

What about slow motion, you may ask? Well the person in the booth at the theater doesn't slow down the speed of the projector on cue. Theaters project film at a standard 24 fps.

Slow motion is when an action appears slowed down while still projected at the standard rate. It might take 4 seconds to watch a guy do a cartwheel in real time. Watching that same action stretched out on film in slow–mo might take 10 seconds of your life. Watching slow motion takes more time. How to capture more time in the same action? More watching time takes more seconds... that means more frames. More frames per second. Aha!

The camera can record more frames than the standard 24 fps, meaning the film runs through the camera faster, taking more pictures of the action. Recording at 48 fps means recording twice as many frames than at 24 fps. Playing back those 48 frames at an equal 48 fps would appear to be in real time speed. Playing those 48 frames at the standard 24 fps, the cartwheel will appear to be at half speed, (or twice as slow as normal). Slow motion!

More frames recorded, more frames to playback.

Fast motion is the opposite. Filming at 12 fps means less frames than the standard 24 per second going through the camera. Meaning playing back at the standard 24 fps, the cartwheel will appear to be twice the speed.

Perhaps its easier to 'splain with **timelapse.** Set a camera that can do timelapse to record 1 frame an hour. After a full day's cycle, 24 hours, we would have 24 frames. It took a whole day and night to record, but all that time and action would be condensed to be only 1 second of footage played at standard speed – 24 frames of sun moon stars dancing across the sky.

VIDEO

Now comes the confusing part. What, only now? Images on the old boxy TV's weren't projected so much as scanned onto the back of the big cathode ray tube. In the US that happened at what is considered 30 frames per second (with alternating lines of scanning, producing 2 fields per frame). So video, or better said digital cameras, run standard at 30 fps.

But not really. It's 29.97.

All of the same principles apply, compared to the standard frame rate.

The faster the camera records the slower the motion appears in playback.

The slower the camera records the faster the motion appears in playback.

With the digital cameras and the computer software now, images can be manipulated in post in different ways. But it makes for a better final image to change frame rates in the camera. Often a Director will film something special at 48 or 60 fps, and if they change their mind the image can be manipulated to appear at 30fps in playback anyway.

CONTINUITY AND HELPING
TO HIDE THE EDIT

Go with the flow, don't break the spell! Movie making is story telling, with the goal to keep the viewer immersed in it. Unless jarring for effect, the smoother and less noticeable the transition between shots, the better. Know the rules then break them with spicy relish when appropriate!

SCREEN DIRECTION

A monitor, or frame, is a rectangle with up, down, left and right sides. So watching the screen, tell an Actor facing the camera to move left (left side of the frame, your left, toward the left side on the rectangle) and he moves to your *right* (his left.) To not diddle away the day in this dance we instead ask the Actor to move CAMERA LEFT. Left for the camera and thus frame (think of the lens as your eye) is still to the Actor's right side but now he understands what's being asked of him.

Part of this smooth flow of editing involves maintaining **screen direction**. This helps the viewer know where the Actors and objects are in relation to one another. Action moves across the screen in the same general direction from one shot to the next.

Imagine a car chase on the screen. See a Wide Shot of The Bandit's Trans Am blast down the highway, moving left to right across the screen. Cut closer to a Full Shot, the car speeds past the camera still going left to right. Bandit says, into his CB radio, "He's hot on our tail!"

Cut to a shot of Smokey in hot pursuit, squad car speeding... going frame right to left. Huh? Wait you're going the wrong way! Or so it would feel. Instead, cut to a shot of Smokey driving in the same direction we've seen the Bandit, left to right, an there's less chance of disorientation.

How about this... See a Wide Shot of Walter and Joe on a football field. They are alone. Joe runs toward the camera, and exits the frame camera right. Cut to a closer shot of Walter as he throws the football to Joe. "Here it comes, Joe!" Except that he throws the ball to camera left. Huh? Is there some mystery person there? Joe ran off on the right side of frame, so the ball should go to the right of frame. Movement goes to the right to Joe, left to Walter.

LOOKLINES

Screen direction is important with looks as well, to keep geography and orientation clear. When speaking to an Actor or Camera Operator we refer to a look line or **eye line**, meaning where the Actor should be looking in the shot, as being:

- **Lens Left** or **Lens Right** - just beside the lens
- **Camera Left** or **Camera Right** – just beside the camera
- **Frame Left** or **Frame Right** - more profile
- **Directly to Lens** – looking into the camera
- **Higher** – as if looking to someone taller
- **Lower** – as if looking to someone shorter

When cutting between two people in a conversation it should appear that they are talking to one another. We must understand where the camera should be in relation to an Actor, and where that Actors should be in relation to one another.

As we go in for coverage, camera moving in closer and closer on a character, we want to make sure the different sized shots will cut together smoothly, and keep the audience on track. So it helps when single shots of different characters are similar in size. But it also helps when the perspective, though we go in closer, is from the same side of "the line."

THE LINE

There's a line of dialogue, and screen direction is a line of movement. Directors and Producers are considered above the line while crumbly crew is below the line. But when film folks ponder THE LINE, this refers to the **180 degree** rule.

The mighty rule - basically, don't cross the line! At least don't cross it on accident.

The line is the axis between two subjects, as in two Actors. It helps our viewing brains to keep a sense of geography when, as per the earlier OTS (over the shoulder) example, Cindy is always seen on the left of frame and Bobby on the right. That gets mixed up when camera crosses the line, also called jumping the line. It can be jarring or disorienting to the viewer.

With digital multi-cam shoots, filming is often run and gun, with axis lines crossed for effect, but it's good to know the "rules" so choices can be made instead of mistakes! The Editor will much appreciate it.

Let us visualize. Or better yet draw a circle. Draw a line across it, like an equator. Lightly shade the top half and leave the bottom half white, presuming you are using white paper. Place two actors on the line, facing one another. Seen from above this would be the top of their heads and shoulders - small circles will suffice to represent them.

Now put a camera in the lower or white half of the circle.

Stay in your hemisphere! Keeping the camera in the white half of the circle will keep you on the correct side of the line for the 2 Shot, Singles or OTS. Half of a circle, 180 degrees fanning out from the center, see?

Camera doesn't literally have to stay in the semi-circle it's just for clarity about being on that side of the world or line.

The next movie or TV night, watch with more awareness and notice how often the 180 degree rule plays out.

Sometimes Directors cross the line on purpose for style, sometimes they might get bamboozled with a limited space or stuck in a doorway in a weird way. Crossing the line isn't so jarring, and is no longer crossing the line, if there's an on screen move that brings the viewer over the line, be it a camera move crossing over or if an actor turns their head or body in a different direction. Or a transition like a cutaway, or a really wide shot or a neutral shot – like if a person walks frame left to right, cut in a frontal shot (them walking to camera), then cross the line from where you started to a shot of that person walking frame right to left.

Piece of cake. Until there are more actors in the space at once, getting overs for multiple characters, and especially when they are moving around.   Then, take it bit by bit, noticing the axis lines between the characters that address one another with dialogue or reactions, for where an actor is for a given part of the scene.

I don't watch football but the little diagrams showing the plays, the players move around and such – thumbs up! This can apply to filming strategy too. As the scene progresses, it's good to keep a quick note of who is where on screen.

CONTINUE WITH CONTINUITY

...As in an uninterrupted succession of story. Concerning film, think of it as matching – objects, action, emotion or editing. When done properly the audience doesn't notice! But when there's a big enough error the flow of story can get broken, even with a subconscious blip of "wait, I thought the coffee mug was in the other hand" or "didn't he already open up the newspaper?"

Sometimes the boo boos slip through while filming, and sometimes choices are made in editing for performance pulled from different takes regardless of variation. Occasionally a film will have a Script Supervisor to take notes as well as a Continuity Supervisor to just make sure everything matches and will cut together.

But that's more moooney, so tis almost always a lonely Script Sup to follow dialogue, write notes, take continuity pictures and track props and action.

ESTABLISHING LOOKS

Looks and props get written into the script, established at a certain scene in the timeline, even if it's subtle and there is no flashing red arrow to point it out. The Script Sup is the arrow and fine tooth comb-er!

Back to the Breakdowns... If on DAY 4 in the story Laura slashes her arm, she would wear a bandage or later have a scar from it in the scenes that take place after DAY 4. The written script may not remind you or mention this ever again, but mighty Script Sup knows, and makes sure Props or Make Up are on the right page at the right time.

REVERSING THE MATCH

Remember, because Productions almost always film out of scene and story order, the first time Laura's cut arm appears on the set to be filmed may not be the first time it appears in the story.

If the slash happens on story DAY 4 but the shooting schedule has a scene with Laura from story DAY 7 up first, the Director must **establish** which arm and where to place the wound on the arm, and there it should remain for all scenes showing it. So when the crew later films the injury happening (DAY 4 in the script and breakdown) it will have to happen on the same spot on the same arm.

THE ARC

There are three arcs of continuity happening at the same time – the whole movie, the scene clusters and the be-here-now scene. This is how I approach a movie or show.

The Whole Enchilada

The Whole Movie, all the way across the board, the scope of the timeline. This is tracking the constants, for example a character that always wears a wedding ring, or glasses, or has to keep up an accent or affectation that is not native to the Actor. This character's cell phone, that character's car usually stays the same - givens that are really not. In the long days/late hours folks can forget or think someone else has double-checked.

Puddle Jumping

Scene Clusters. Some things have to match specific scenes,

which may be sequential or scattered throughout the film. And which may be filmed back to back, or on separate shooting days or separate locations. Typically wardrobe is assigned to particular story days, and props may be too. Because we often film out of order, at times we must reverse the match.

There are things to match visually, but **emotions** need to match as well. Script reads that Jethro storms through the house, angry. You mad, Bro? Say on Monday we film the scene of him leaving the kitchen in anger to answer a ringing phone. The next scene in the script has him answer the phone in the bedroom. But that is filmed days later at a different location.

Although in reality the sequential direct-cut scenes are being filmed days apart in different locations, we must ensure Jethro's wardrobe, hair and make up, and emotional state match in the finished film to make it seem like he walked directly from one room to the next.

Here's another way that breakdown comes in handy. When filming a given scene it's good practice to find the previous and then the following scripted scene an Actor is in. This is part of the Actor's homework for any internal beats they have, but schedules can move fast or change and it helps the Script Sup to remember if there's a prop or emotional flow to match or consider.

Actor - "Where am I coming from (in the story)?"
Prepared Script Sup - "You threw a punch at your uncle in the deli. This scene takes place just after that."

Be Here Now, And Now, And Now

Each Scene. Before cameras roll Script Sup checks that wardrobe, H/MU and props match any already established look. Reference pictures captures detail - how the hat was tilted, shirt buttoned, sleeves were rolled up, which ring on which finger. Those Wardrobe Outlines come in handy too.

And does lighting match – headlights on, desk lamp on, Christmas lights on? Sunny vs. cloudy, long vs. short shadows? In the reset when changing camera angles things can move or get turned off. This is the DP's domain and sometimes it's catch as catch can, but its good to be aware, no? Yes!

Pictures of the set are also useful, as furniture and even walls gets shuffled around as we go in for coverage. Set Dec should take set pictures, but it's good to have your own for reference just in case.

ROLLING AND THE SIDES

While cameras roll I take chicken scratch notes for self on the Sides, or on my digital script then clean up the pages before sending them in. Just for self I scribble out a map or blueprint of the scene (and each set up if they differ) following who, what, when and where. I'll be extra honest here, with several cameras on several Actors doing variations each take, sometimes it can feel like chasing a train, and a little drawing or arrow indicating an Actor's movement several takes back can be a lifeline.

WHO

Which Actor is the note for? Remember lining the script pages per camera set up? I roughly line the Sides too. In a Two Shot I scribble notes for the actor on frame left to the left of the line, actor on frame right to the right of it. If several actors have business usually a first initial per character suffices.

WHAT

What is the prop? Not just a glass of tea, but a glass that is only half full at the start of the scene, or a cigarette that is barely burnt. If a take 'picks up' from the middle of a scene are the levels of the drink or cigarette correct? Which hand does the Actor use? How does he hold the glass?

WHEN

When in the scene, where in dialogue does something worth matching occur? David leans back at his dialogue line "What do you mean?" Margaret rises on "It's over." He slams the glass down when she begins to cry.

Sometimes the edit point is a **cut on action.** The Editor will cut from a Medium Shot to a Close Up during Margaret's rise, so it's important to have moves or actions match set up to set up.

WHERE

Where does the actor turn or move to in the frame, with look lines or physically walking about the set? A character may turn (to his left or his right?) to speak to someone off screen for a given set up, or may move out of frame.

Even if Actors don't saunter around the set, things can shift around A LOT during a scene, like hands and hair, or where things end up on a table. Arms crossed go to hands in pockets go to left hand on hip. If there's a cut on action to a closer shot or even doing an OTS where arm position is noticeable, it's helpful to know if for most takes the arms were crossed or elbows on the table for a certain chunk of dialogue.

Long hair is awesome but people forget how pretty tight, slick buns can be. And I hear bonnets are making a comeback – spread the word. Sometimes Actors play with their hair (stop it!)

and sometimes wind or just the wandering through the scene can move it around, so we track when its over one shoulder, behind an ear, all the way back.

If the Director loves a take during which the hair fell forward on the right side for the second half of the scene – going in for close ups, if it doesnt seem to happen naturally, try to match to that, at least for some of the takes.

This is where the Four Colored Pen comes in handy. Each take's scratchy notes and cues and drawings written in a different color help to quickly track which take she sat with her hand on her chin, or which take he took his cowboy hat off late. I scratch on paper but the same can apply if using a tablet.

ANTICIPATE

Looking at the breakdown, noting props, checking the related scenes per Actor and plain old remembering keeps the Script Sup ahead of the game. This particular Character always wears glasses and has a red-cased cell phone. That particular Character has a blue backpack whenever she arrives or leaves the job. Suzy Q dives into the backyard pool in scene 8, and so her hair should still be damp when she makes lunch a short story-while later in scene 12. In a fist fight Steven gets a black eye in scene 30 and the bruise should lighten by scene 45 which is several days later in story time.

CATCHING THE BEATS

Did we cover the whole scene? Did we get everything on the shot list? Did we get every line of dialogue on camera? In close up too?

In the margin of the sides I mark down the special parts in each scene, be it a particular action or an object mentioned that sounds like it will need some emphasis. A busy scene can have so much going on, this serves as a kind of checklist...the key shaking in the lock...the file marked INSURANCE...the feet tip toeing...the gun goes off...dialing 911.

Since the lights are up and the set is dressed to film Jethro picking up the phone, it might be easier to catch an insert of the phone's screen in his hand "now" instead of moving lights and cameras elsewhere only to move it all back after shooting the meat of the scene. The less moving equipment back and forth the more time saved.

Or it can be easy to grab elsewhere, just an ECU of the phone screen that DP will match the lighting to.

Or it might not be a priority, just an extra shot to grab if there's time after getting all the dialogue, and if there's no time to film the phone insert it's OK.

Or it's important enough to owe the insert phone shot and schedule it for another day. If it's a vital part of the scene, Script Sup may hold back 1/8 of the scene's page count value and mark the scene as incomplete. Meaning a scene that's 7/8 of a page would be credited only 6/8 for the day's work, holding back the last 1/8 until filming the phone insert. It's put on Script Sup's running Owe List, and on the Daily Report so the ADs know to schedule that shot in another day.

NEGOTIATING: LET'S GET TO WORK, AND GET PAID FAIRLY...EVENTUALLY

SHOW ME THE MONEY

Different projects have different budgets. The more experience gained, the more say in what pay rate you will accept. Or demand, demand it! But sometimes A-Team crew donates time to small projects as a favor, to encourage the next generation of filmmakers, or just because they love film. So any level of production can potentially expose you to any level of film professional.

Someone already established in the commercial film community in another capacity, if well liked, and well versed in set protocol and job duties, *and* friendly with the Script Sup may be allowed to shadow, then to fill in a day here or there as a splinter unit Script Supervisor on a bigger show.

But most of us started working for free as we learned on the job. Ya gotta give it away to ultimately get something in return. People love film, have stories to tell, and when starting out need all the help they can get!

BUDGETS AND LEVELS OF PRODUCTION
How to start from the outside? One can scan Craig's List,

the State's Film Office, and peek at local Casting or Acting Sites to see what's around. Maybe the University has an electronic bulletin board. Is there a Film or Artist's Co-op in the vicinity?

No Budget, No Pay

Student Films are a great way to put that little toe in the water and put learning into practice. "Will provide a copy of the film and a credit on IMDB" (if you don't know IMDB search for it on the internets). Hey that's more than you started with! If mistakes are going to be made, well, might as well make them where everyone else is messing up too! And where it might be easier to step back and correct those boo boos. But more than likely, there's a slow enough pace to really concentrate and get the basics down. Less expectation, much appreciation.

Some cities also host 48 Hour Film Festivals, where teams of film lovers try their hand at making a short film off the cuff in just 48 hours. That's a fun, and exhausting, way to try on many hats AND have your work officially screened.

Low Budget, No Pay

There still may be no check cashing here, but often at this level a deal's made for **DEFERRED PAY**. If the film's a big hit and gets bought at a festival, the Production comes back to pay the crew at a previously agreed amount per day of work. The Production might be able to cover a teeny small stipend for a kit rental or fuel reimbursement – doesn't hurt to ask.

Also at this level there may be more professional equipment and people with more experience. If a feature, what an opportunity to really sink those teeth into tracking continuity, navigating notes, practicing a script breakdown and being a part of a more developed crew in action.

Low Budget, Low Pay

Movin' on up! Equipment, crew and process SHOULD be getting closer to commercial production than the Student Film days. And now there may be a familiar face on the crew, or perhaps eventually up and coming Actors in the cast.

Also at this level there should be some sort of **DEAL MEMO** made between you and the show, a written contract agreeing on terms of payment, any rentals and such. The bigger the show, the bigger the pile of start paperwork!

The **FLAT RATE** comes into play here. This is a set amount of money per day, not a rate per hour. So the pay is the same for working 10 hours or for working 14. Receiving $100 a day honing those skills at something you love is way better than just a baloney sandwich. And at this level there may be a small kit rental as well.

Indies

When Independent Film became a genre more than a financial status it seemed to attract more established Actors and more money. I see it as a middle ground between Low Budget flexibility and the rigid machine of Union Contract Films.

On Low-Budget and Non-Union Indies nothing is standard. Everything is subject to negotiation. There are certain accepted thresholds in terms of rates, and a Production needs to offer a certain level of pay to get a crew member of a certain caliber and experience.

With Indies, the pay can more closely reflect a Union Scale with either a decent flat rate, or a fair hourly rate. There may be room in the budget for kit rental, camera bump and overtime. What you probably will never ever see is funding going to pension, insurance or dues.

Speaking of Union dues...

THE UNION LABEL

The International Alliance of Theatrical and Stage Employees, IATSE, is a labor union "representing tens of thousands of technicians, artisans and crafts persons in the entertainment industry, including live theatre, motion picture and television production, and trade shows." It is more commonly referred to as IATSE, the IA or the Union, covering the United States and Canada.

By contracting with the Union, a Production agrees to fair wages and working conditions, safety standards and providing benefits. Between the IA for crew, and the various Guilds, as for Actors, Directors, Writers and Producers, if a film has enough of a budget, these groups will want some of that budget to care for their members and organizations beyond hourly pay.

To join the Union, traditionally you must prove you've worked so many days on a Union show in some qualified capacity, then pay an up front initiation fee – save those pennies! This fee includes the first year of dues.

OR work on an Indie that goes Union during Production and that initial fee is waived (woohoo!).

Union members must pay quarterly dues and a Union production diverts a percentage out of each paycheck – make sure to fill out the form that allows them to do so.

Some states are Right To Work, where a person is not obligated to join a Union to hold what may only be a Union job elsewhere. The state I live in is so. But from what I understand, a Union show is supposed to hire Union members first. If they run out of available Union members then they can hire non-members without grief, and those non-members are subject to the same treatment and pay scale as the Union members, without the dues or the benefits.

Under the IA banner stand Local chapters around North America, and the Area Standard Agreements may differ from region to region. For example, the standard pay rate for Union members in Los Angeles will be more than for members in Oklahoma.

Lets get back to it. Low Budget Union films are broken into three levels. As of this writing, according to the 2017-2019 Low Budget Theatrical Agreement, it breaks down as follows.

> Tier 1 – up to $6,000,000
> Tier 2 - $6,000,001 – 10,000,000
> Tier 3 - $10,000,001 – 14,200,000

For low budget that's still a lotta icing on the cake! And budgets go up from there into the ridiculous. Typically crew on a Union show has an 8 hour guarantee (even if you work only 3 hours you still get paid for 8), with time and a half after 8 hours of work, and double time after 14. The base pay rates change with the tiers, but sometimes those rates are negotiable for Keys, which includes Script Supervisor.

NEGOTIATING

OK, say you have a few projects under your belt. A new show's coming to town. You submit a resume, or as you get more established, a movie gets a referral for awesome you and calls to check on your availability. If they are not oozing with details, ask questions! And if it doesn't feel right to be blatant about budget and such, do a little dance. Is there any rapport to be had here?

Ask in a friendly and conversational way! What follows is our side of the conversation...

Can you tell me more about the film? Oh, Werewolves. (means night work).

How many cameras? Three, that's great, you can knock out all that coverage (that's a lot of money in camera crew).

Who's the Director, would I recognize her work? First time, what good fortune (you may be teaching *them!* Extra work or extra fun for you).

Gee that sounds like a big story, is this a Union show? Oh, Tier 2 (this gives you a budget range and you know they have a standard rate they must meet).

Or be blunt and direct! *What's the budget? Who's attached to the project? How's the schedule?*

If they feel you are the right person for the job, a talk with the Director or another Producer may be arranged first, or it may go straight into negotiating. You may read the script before the next phase of negotiating. They may present an offer, or ask for your rate.

Most of the time, this is just a starting point.

Io sono Italiano. And in Italian the word for a store or a shop is *negozio,* (like negotiate, see?) where people work out a deal to make an exchange for what each perceives as having value.

If they are shopping around, a Producer is looking to hire the best Script Supervisor for the least expense they can get away with. A Production wants someone knowledgeable, with appropriate experience and a suitable personality.

And ya know what? We don't have any department overhead of gear, work trucks, having to hire crew or cost them "man" days. A good Script Supervisor will SAVE a Production money with every error we catch, every opportunity we spot to grab an owed insert or Voice Over, every moment we can help an Actor rehearse, every time we can explain what's not working in a shot.

A Script Sup wants the best deal rate, for the least aggravation! Fair compensation for time and skill. But part of the package may be in gaining more experience working with new technology or with certain people. Parameters can be different for different folks. Know what's realistic, as well as what you need and what you need to walk away from.

EXTRA EXTRA

Before cutting to the rate chase, there are several "extras" (really necessities) to be aware of, to pipe up about. Union shows expect to cover these, but still ask and clarify, don't presume (some Producers will try to get away with every penny they can). Indies will often accommodate some as well.

Prep Days Baseline

We need 2 days for an hour long TV show, 2.5 for a TV Pilot, 5 days plus for a feature (low budget may push for compromise here). They tend to be charged at 10 hours per day. Meetings for Television especially can eat all your prep so after 1 production meeting, if requested to attend concept and tone meetings, those 10 hour prep days might become 12 or an extra day altogether.

Timing

I charge a flat rate here, more for a feature, but basically this equals at least a separate, additional day of prep.

Kit Rental

Whether using a tablet on set or a computer at home for

breakdowns and such, these electronics are part of our tool kit and a production will often budget for this ($10 – 25 per workday is what I've been seeing for awhile). Includes prep days.

Camera Bump

More than 1 camera means more notes, more camera reports, more monitors to track, more 2nd ACs to chase down, more WORK! Any day with more than 1 camera rolling on our watch gets a bump in pay - $40 total per day (for all cameras total not per additional) in this neck of the woods.

Mileage

A lot of location work can mean a lot of driving. Every mile past a certain radius from the center of the city or the production office should be compensated.

Wrap Out

I'll ask for a day or 2 of wrap on a typical movie, with TV not so much. Now with digital systems, wrap out is quicker. Wrap means cleaning up, organizing and presenting the completed lined script with left-hand pages, the daily reports and shot lists in day order, continuity pictures or wardrobe outline, the script breakdown and a list of what's owed (thus what scenes are not complete and why). With paper the office gets the originals.

This is different from the standard hour added at the end of each work day for wrap out and prep for the following workday.

A Production depends on this "wrap book" when later there's a reshoot or even a re-edit. If they don't value the extra time it takes to neatly prepare all of this, I still send the completed script in with the last day's notes (one extra file to send, no biggie). But the potentially way-down-the-road editorial department will have to sift through each shooting days report notes, which are with the production office, for further info.

DISTANT HIRE

Working out of state, beyond the coverage of the Local, on a Union show one should be considered a Distant Hire. There's extra paperwork needed to ensure benefits go to the right place.

Working within your Local, within your home state but away from a production city must in many ways be considered a distant hire as well. But even a non-Union show will have to provide more than just an hourly rate. Never presume, clarify! Each Union project has a Contract, and specific changes may be written in that vary from the Standard Agreemants.

That being said Script Sup can (try to) negotiate for something different. We'll get to that in a bit.

Travel

This is paid time to drive or fly to production, a 4 hour minimum each way. Fuel should be reimbursed or plane tickets (and cab fare to airport) provided. Also any luggage fees.

Transportation

Meaning a rental car, production van rides, or fuel receipt reimbursement when self driving. Did I ever tell you about the time a show gave me a car so small I couldn't fit my luggage in it?

Housing

A hotel or a realistic stipend must be provided. It's tricky figuring out housing in an unfamiliar place, especially without knowing where all the filming locations are, or the wrong parts of town. But self-housing can sometimes mean more stipend money in pocket. Local folks in the Production office might have recommendations.

You'd think a gal from out of town would not have to say this out loud to a Producer, but I have now learned to stipulate a clean, safe hotel room, preferably where camera crew is staying (vs. where some shows may put the Transpo crew - unfortunately there can be a big difference). Rest is important and safety numero uno.

Per Diem

Daily cash to cover meals not provided on set, so for "dinner" during production days, and for 3 squares each day off.

Portal to Portal

As a Distant Hire, the individual call and wrap times should reflect driving time between the hotel and the set, for call time and wrap, whether it's a self-drive or van pick up. If Production covers portal to portal make sure to keep this straight with the AD making the call sheet.

Idle Days

That's 4 hours pay per day off, because we are stuck away from our own lovely beddy by.

AND NOW BACK TO MAKING THE DEAL

If the Producer can't or won't budge on the rate even after showing them the experience, reputation, good humor, degrees or certificates, and interest we bring to the table, remember those several "extra" categories that should be part of the deal and may help to compensate. Perhaps some creative budget juggling would supply an extra day of prep, a bigger kit rental, or a local Production covering a couple fuel receipts to bump up the bottom line of pay.

Friendly reminder of another dash for cash – schedules change, life happens, sometimes a show needs a replacement ASAP. A last minute emergency call for work that same day or the next morning calls for a last minute emergency higher rate!

Know yourself, your line of what you need, what's acceptable and what is not. If the rate seems low for the budget and what I have to offer a show, I'll tell the Producer we're off to a good start, and I'd like to work something out we are both comfortable with. Then I'll ask if she would look at the numbers again with her superpowers activated to see what more Production can do, and let's touch base later.

Meanwhile they can call around looking for someone else, or if honorable they will try to bring even a little more to the table. Or they may flat out say "take it or leave it." And if your gut tells you to leave it, pay attention to that too. If a problem arises during production, it's much nicer with folks that aim to make things work, than with someone that's inflexible and can't be bothered.

Always clarify what you are asking for and what you understand is agreed upon. Email is a great written way to verify that you and the Producer are on the same page. From the first day of work it can take 2 weeks to get a paycheck -a lot of time to invest in a project before learning there's a communication problem about your deal!

TIMECARDS

Once on a paying gig, there's a contract and start paperwork to fill out with Production before (OK, maybe during) the first day of filming, again clarifying that deal on paper. Then at the end of each week fill out a timecard (or an invoice if asked).

By the end of the following work week the checks come out. On a bigger show we tell the 2nd AD our out times each day, but also keep track for oneself and still turn in a timecard.

Timecard hours are broken into 6 minute increments (10 increments to an hour = 60 minutes) and military time, which is a 24 hour day, not 12 hours a.m. and 12 hours p.m. Midnight before work is Zero, and we go up from there - 1 a.m. is 1, 8 a.m. is 8. Noon is 12. Four p.m. is 16.

Midnight at the end of work is 24, and we are still going up - 1 a.m. at the end of the work shift is 25.

So call at 8 a.m. is 8.0. Wrap out time at 8:00 pm is 20.0. (12 noon + 8 more hours= 20). Thus 8 p.m. translates to 20 hours out from the Midnight.

Wrap out time at 8:24 p.m. is 20.4. The point 4 means 4 blocks out of the 10 of those 6 minute increments (4 blocks x 6 minutes = 24 minutes). If personal wrap out time is not on the nose of a 6 minute interval, round up to the next interval!

NOT YOUR FIRST TIME TO THE RODEO

I'm not crazy about saying no to a serious job offer, but after getting the details sometimes a project is just NOT the right thing at the time. So what would it take to have a go at it - more money, extra prep, a better stipend, a rental car? Put it on the table as what you would need to give your best to a particular project and it's in their court. They can pass and you haven't said no, or they give you all this cherry sprinkles and icing you've asked for, showing they honor you, and maybe it won't be so bad after all!

Now, make it so!

SELF CARE

As a department of one, knowing the ins and outs of the script and established continuity, there is a particular commandment for the Script Supervisor: "Thou shalt not get sick enough to miss work." And believe me, despite any inconvenience, it is easier to *stay* healthy than to *get* healthy.

Even when it's easy, production is hard. Strong-willed and talented crew members choose to join the film army, and from there choices are then made *for* us. We are told where and what time to report for duty each day. We are told when to break for lunch and what to eat. We are told who we are going to work with and on what material. We are told when to film by day, and when to film overnight. We are told when we can be dismissed, and may get a full weekend's R&R, or only 1 day.

Working on set can be referred to as being in the trenches. It's a battle to make our day, stay on schedule, and with many disparate (some times desperate, if you get on a rough project) hands, make movie magic, often under pressure.

At home I can wake, eat, nap, stretch, snack, rest, move inside or outside, put attention on work or play, and pee luxuriously at my leisure. I can go to bed any ole time I want.

Unfortunately, this alone does not pay.

Production work requires stamina for the big picture – weeks or months of long hours, shifting schedules, eating differently than you might usually, at all times of day or night, not enough sleep, too much tension, too much coffee, exposure to the elements or not so healthy locations, staying in strange hotels, limited recharge time with family, friends and pets.

No matter how young or in shape you are when the Director first calls "Action!" if you work on grueling and intense shows enough times, well, you just might not be so young and in shape when you come out the other side at picture wrap.

And this can be a slippery slope, waiting 'til the show's over to hit the gym, or eat better. Studio or soundstage work in a controlled environment and more regular hours can make a difference in maintaining health for sure.

LOVE what you are doing. And to keep on doing it, prepare and protect yourself, physically and emotionally.

BODY EVERYBODY

No matter where the Script Supervisor works - sitting by the monitors, climbing into a process trailer, running on to the set to make a correction – the brain power must also be on full speed. This brain goes to 11!

We don't want body or beautiful mind to be crashing, or weak, or in pain. Give yourself the best chance possible for success and stamina. Some suggestions...

Water

Not soda, not coffee, not juice. Herbal tea gets a pass. Carbonation, the CO_2, even in sparkling water, can mess up digestion. Drink drink drink mostly water. Thirst means you're behind, don't get to that point. Say no to headaches. In the heat and in the cold, HYDRATE!!! BTW, it may be worth looking at a water filter for your kitchen.

Eat Well

Make the best food choices you can. Yes sample some of the treats, but eating full out Gas Station Style (chips, cookies, candy, donuts) will leave your long-term tank empty. Despite it feeling like stop and go at times, film production is not a sprint but more of a cross-country run.

Stay Regular

How to say.... Poop. This is the main way the body expels toxins. With different eating and sleeping schedules our bodies can get turned around, and there probably won't be a convenient time to porcelain play a couple relaxing rounds of Sudoku between set ups.

Before bedtime some vitamin C, magnesium, a wee few drops of castor oil if desperate, or even a hot Epsom salt bath can help the body relax and take care of business at home on a regular basis instead of trying to go boom boom in a closet on wheels while cameras reload, wearing your headphones to listen for how close you are to shooting.

Heard it from a friend.

Sleep

Monday's alarm might be set for 5:00 am. By that Friday, the alarm may be set for 5:00 pm. Does anyone really get used to that? Plan to get as much restful sleep as possible. Set yourself up for success. After work, wrap and prep, but if feeling sleepy it can be better to rest, then wake a little early to prep in the morning. Don't use electronics right before bed, try to make the bedroom dark and quiet. Sleep mask and ear plugs anyone? Hot baths help. Gentle natural plant based sleep aides are out there. A dreamy meditation podcast or relaxing music while taking slow deep breaths can help too.

And here's a big one – try turning the WiFi off for sleep. Go ahead, try it for a few nights and see if you rest more deeply.

Supplements

It may be worth investing in the highest quality vitamins possible. During production a lot is asked of our bodies, and our vitamins and minerals can get depleted, so why not fill in some of those gaps?

Along with a clean liquid all-in-one, I add Lutein for tired eyes (from hours of staring at script and screen), Vitamin C to boost immunity, Magnesium and Potassium to keep the Charlie Horses at bay. I try to take these goodies twice a day. Activated Charcoal stays on hand for sour tummy. What works for you?

Clothing

Weather Proof. When filming on location, be prepared for unexpected climate or weather. Can you fit something extra in your bag? No harm in keeping a hat, coat, raingear and boots in the car or on the camera truck. Don't skimp, protect yourself with gear that will really keep you dry, keep you warm, block the sun – whatever's needed when in the wild!

By the way, sound stages can be shockingly hot or unbearably cold too.

To a degree, we teach people how to treat us, and part of that is with how we dress. For safety **always** wear close-toed shoes, but from there it's up to you. Aim to be comfortable and also appropriate, professional. When I'm trying to communicate I want people to listen and look in my eyes, not my bewbs. Dress like a hoochie and you may not be taken as seriously. Look like a slob, you risk getting treated like a slob. I tend to wear simple blouses and jeans. Respect my authori-tay! What's your style?

By the way, we do a lot of location shooting in these parts. I quickly learned it does not pay (or it *does* pay – the store and the cleaners) to wear a nice new $$$ pair of jeans or shirt just to have them destroyed while filming in a field of mud or in a quarry or a sewage plant. Apart from weather gear, I thrift and go garage saling for my work clothes, getting clean like-new pieces for pennies on the dollar.

Stretch

It helps to loosen up in the morning and to relieve the day's tension in the evening. Exaggerated shoulder shrugs, shaking your arms in the air, trunk twists, lunges, and even hanging head and shoulders off of the bed can help keep from getting too crunchy!

◆ ◆ ◆

THE WOO WOO IN YOU YOU

PROTECT YOUR SELF

We are each infinite consciousness on a spiritual journey having a human experience. IMHO. We constantly engage in, create and are exposed to psychic energy. And I don't mean mind reading, though some folks are perhaps sensitive in that sort of way.

Between the different people, the subject matter of any given project and the various locations, we as humans can be affected, for good and not so good, by our surroundings. Working with toxic people, a vile story or unhealthy conditions long enough can bring anyone down and even effect precious time off. Ever been there?

In production there can be a lot of money, power and ego playing out in unhealthy ways, and even if you do not engage in it, that vibe can soil your beautiful and vibrant energy if you are not careful. Tuning it out can only get you so far – if it affects the rest of the crew it affects you.

While doing the best possible for physical health, it's important to protect your psyche on the job as well. Some suggestions...

Intentions

Wake up and be grateful, another day to get it right or make it even better! Set the tone, tell YOUniverse the type of day you expect – productive, time flies, full of opportunity. Plant those feet on the floor and ground yourself to something wonderful.

We have forgotten how powerful we are. If you wake up and play into a grouchy "Oh Funk" mind set, chances are more likely you will have an "Oh Funk" sort of day. So why not wake up and play into "Oh Yay!"?

Aura

Perhaps heart energy is another way to look at this field that surrounds each of us. At home, let it all hang out, Baby. But in the world, especially at work, I want to protect myself from drama, ego, power plays, and other people's negativity. So I envision and physically act out zipping up my aura, up my front and down my back. On the way to work I remember to surround myself, and the car, in a bubble of white light.

So if you see a glowing egg driving down the road, it's me.

But wait, there's more. After work, in the shower, I imagine scrubbing away any yucky stuff from the day, cleaning anything that might cloud my bright beautiful aura.

Silly you say? Maybe. But maybe we create what we think,

and maybe what we put our attention on really does grow, so why not remind ourselves we are worthy of protection and positivity?

Zip The Lips

No gossip. Nope. Script Supervisor often has access to the conversation of Actors, Directors, Producers and Writers. Even if they are not including you in a particular conversation, if you hear something private keep it to yourself.

This also applies to below the line - you may come across fellow crew members on future projects, don't risk bad blood. When people are tired it's too easy to speak about low level things, whisper in the corners about other folks out of frustration or amusement. Take the high road, we are a film family and live by a certain code.

Instead of tearing each other down lets build each other up! This does not mean we don't share funny stories, observations, problems to be solved or let one another blow off a little steam – but believe me, it's better for YOUR state of mind to not participate in the big G.

Breathe

Shallow breathing can put the body in a state of stress. Deep breathing can relax or revive, tis amazing!

Wake up...! A few (loud) rounds of inhaling through the nose with a slow thorough exhale out of the mouth can revive a tired Script Supervisor in mere moments, instead of drinking a 4 a.m. cup of Joe that will kick in just as you put your head to the pillow a couple hours later. More oxygen going more deeply to that sluggish blood deprived brain!

Ready? Set? Go Get 'Em!

EPILOGUE

Thank you so much for reading along and spending precious time. Obviously you are curious and willing to learn or understand something new, and that's rather wonderful!

Now that we are friends it is time for the truth. Technically... I am not a Script Supervisor. To clarify, Script Supervising is what I do, it is not who I am. Shows come and go, careers come and go, lifetimes within this lifetime come and go. Who I am is not tied to what I do, but to how I do, be it running lines with an Actor, or shooing chickens out of the garden. Hopefully always growing in kindness, strength, discernment and peace.

Bless you on your journey of discovering and forming who *you* are too!

loveb

REFUND POLICY

There is no refund policy. Thank you for your generous donation to the Beatrice Bellino Script Supervisor Retirement Fund. Now you might as well roll up your sleeves and get back to it!

By the way, there also is no Beatrice Bellino Script Supervisor Retirement Fund, that is a joke, a joke! But your support IS much appreciated.

Made in the USA
Coppell, TX
29 April 2021

54760186R00066